The Paris Shopping Companion

The Paris Shopping Companion

A PERSONAL GUIDE
TO THE FINEST SHOPS IN PARIS
FOR EVERY POCKETBOOK

Second Edition

Susan Swire Winkler

CUMBERLAND HOUSE PUBLISHING
NASHVILLE, TENNESSEE

The original edition of this book was published in the United States in 1993 by Cobble & Mickle Books.

Published by Cumberland House Publishing, Inc., 431 Harding Industrial Drive, Nashville, Tennessee 37211-3160.

Cover design by Tonya Presley.
Text design by Julie Pitkin.

Library of Congress Cataloging-in-Publication Data

Winkler, Susan Swire, 1950—
    The Paris shopping companion : a personal guide to the finest shops in Paris for every pocketbook / Susan Swire Winkler.—2nd ed.
        p.   cm.
    Includes index.
    ISBN 1–888952–70–9 (pbk. : alk. paper)
    1. Shopping—France—Paris—Guidebooks. 2. Paris (France)—Guidebooks.   I. Title.
TX337.F82P3793   1998
380.1'450002544361—dc21   98–13934
                                                    CIP

Printed in the United States of America
3 4 5 6 7 8 — 01 00

To my family,

who never tires of tales of shopping and Paris,

and especially Julia,

my shopping companion.

Acknowledgments

Margie Adams, Michele Buc, Micheline Fried, Yvonne Gionnet, Laurie Harper, Lauren Heller, Julie Jayne, Clotilde Landolfini, Luiza Leite, Randy Lombard, Lori McNeese, Rebecca Newman, Julie Pitkin, Ron Pitkin, Tonya Presley, Jordan Winkler, Jacob Winkler, and the shopkeepers of Paris . . . without whom there would be no book.

Contents

Introduction

Ever since I saw the movie *Gigi* as a young girl, I have been fascinated by the French and the French way of life. As a student abroad in Paris, as a graduate student in French literature, as a fashion journalist and as an importer of French linens for my own shop, I have pursued the enigma that is French style.

I still see Paris through an overlay of *Gigi*, with an eye to what is undeniably and irresistibly French in a city that is being invaded, like the rest of the sophisticated world, with the so-called international style.

The Paris Shopping Companion is a very personal account of Paris as I see it, shop by shop. Concentrating on what is French by origin or adoption, it is a customized guide that explains how to look at each establishment from a French point of view, as much as a primer that suggests what to buy at each stop along the way.

To arrive in Paris and take in everything at once can be confusing, if not overwhelming. In this book I have tried to sort out the best of the best, choosing my favorite shops and pointing out the smartest buys in a variety of price ranges. I have made a special effort to highlight wise purchases in even the most expensive shops. These often make the most distinctive gifts because they come so beautifully wrapped and packaged.

To the French, shopping is a cultivated activity. Window-shopping is considered a respectable, even edifying pastime. It seems that all of Paris is out and about on weekends and warm evenings, taking time to enjoy the beauty of the city, to discuss the latest changes in the windows of their neighborhood shops, or to critique the newest *couture* fashions along the boulevards. In the realm of design, all Parisians are experts. They became so by studying the streets and shops of the city, and following the news in a culture where fashion shows make the front page and the editorials.

Within a few minutes of arriving in the city, you'll recognize the latest styles. Simply park yourself at your hotel window or in a cafe and study the self-assured *Parisienne* as she passes by. What is she wearing and how is she wearing it? You'll soon realize that the woman on the street has a savvy that fashion magazines envy. To obtain some of that *savoir-faire* yourself, adopt her air of confidence and set out to find exactly what you've seen and liked. Or find a shop you admire and let the adept sales help put everything together for you.

You can tour Paris, study Paris, or just walk Paris. But it's shopping Paris that may be the most pleasant and enlightened way to get to know the city, and even those who hate shopping love it in Paris. Even those with little money to spend find their shopping hours well spent. In a culture where style of life is a source of national pride and pleasure, shopping as the French do is an invaluable approach to understanding French culture. All the better if you can take some of that culture home with you.

Susan Swire Winkler

Practical Matters

WHEN TO GO

Paris is a pleasure any time of year, but die-hard shoppers may want to avoid the period from mid-July to the end of August, when many shops and restaurants are closed while their owners and staff are *en vacances* (on vacation) with most of their countrymen. It is always a good idea to check with your local French Consulate beforehand for dates of holidays when shops and banks will be closed.

WHAT TO TAKE

Walking shoes, a detailed street map (I recommend the pocket-size Michelin plan #14), calculator (non-solar), credit cards (must include Visa), automatic teller machine cards, traveler's checks in French francs and in dollars, and at least one empty suitcase for carrying your purchases home.

As a matter of course, I always keep my money, credit cards, and passport concealed under my clothing in a small, flat purse that hangs from my neck.

GETTING AROUND

A city this beautiful is best seen on foot. I heartily recommend a good pair of walking shoes and your map on all but the most rushed or inclement day. When you must, take a taxi (expensive) or the highly efficient *métro* (subway system). It is economical to buy a *carnet* (packet of ten tickets) for first (only an advantage during rush-hour) or second-class travel. The bus is fine, and accepts métro tickets, but it's slower and more difficult to figure out, and you must indicate to the driver when you want to be let off.

CASH AND CREDIT

You are assured the best rate of exchange, the inter-bank rate, when you pay by credit card. Paying by credit card also gives you a clear record of your purchases and expedites your *détaxe* (tax reimbursement). Most Parisian establishments accept Visa (known as Carte Bleue in France) and you shouldn't leave yours at home. Remember that there may be a rate fluctuation between the time you purchase and the time your transaction is processed in a bank.

Always bring traveler's checks in French francs and in dollars so you'll have some local currency when you arrive and still be able to obtain the most current exchange rate in Paris. It is smart to cash your dollar traveler's checks every two to three days, as needed, to avoid bringing home extra francs that you must then pay to reconvert to dollars.

Handle your currency exchanges in a local bank (you can shop around for the best rate), which traditionally offers better values than change booths and hotels.

You may be able to draw francs at a good rate directly from your checking account by using your automatic teller machine card in France. Check with your bank before you go for locations of automatic teller machines in Paris that will take your card.

TAX REFUNDS

As a tourist, you are entitled to a tax refund (*détaxe*) for purchases totaling at least 1,200F in one store. If you are shopping with a friend, you may combine your purchases to achieve the total, and share the refund back home. Refunds vary from 12 to 33 percent, with most at about 13 percent, depending on the item. You can more or less make up for your import duty on the same items by following the *détaxe* procedure. (Note that *détaxe* does not apply to antiques.)

When you shop, be sure to have your passport and the proper name and address of your hotel or residence in Paris handy. Request the *détaxe* forms, which the store will fill out with your help in a matter of minutes. You will leave the shop with your *détaxe* forms in a stamped envelope addressed to the shop. If you have paid for your purchases by credit card your refund will appear in dollars as a credit to your card's account; otherwise you will be mailed a refund check in French francs. Either way takes about three months.

If you pay by credit card the boutique sometimes offers to write up one purchase slip that includes the tax to be refunded and a second purchase slip with the tax already deducted. In this case, when you have processed your *détaxe* forms upon departing France, the shop will tear up the first slip and you won't have to wait for a refund.

When you are leaving the country (at the airport or train station), go to the customs official at the *bureau de détaxe* before you check your luggage—he may want to inspect your purchases. He will stamp your documents, keep one copy, and return one copy for you to mail on the spot in the store envelope, and one copy for you to keep (the green one). When the store receives your mailed copy, the refund process begins.

Don't let the *détaxe* process worry you. It's well worth the little effort and it always works.

SHIPPING AND CARRYING YOUR PURCHASES HOME

The simplest and cheapest way to get your purchases back home is to carry them with you in the extra suitcase(s) you prudently packed. I always travel to France with my second-largest luggage piece packed and inside my otherwise empty largest luggage, and return home with both pieces filled. I also take an empty nylon athletic bag or two. Be sure to check with your airline on your luggage allowance.

Be aware right off that the cost of shipping large pieces home may change your mind about making the purchase. Shipping is appropriate when you know you'll never find the same thing in the States or don't want to look for it again, and you are comfortable with the associated costs. A reliable seller should help you arrange shipping and give you the exact costs beforehand.

Smaller items can be shipped by some stores. Again, get a firm shipping price. Ocean transport takes about twice the time at half the cost of air shipment. For items shipped directly from the store, the *détaxe* is automatically deducted without paperwork on your part.

Any post office offers reliable shipping at good rates. Bring your parcel in fully packaged and wait your turn.

U.S. CUSTOMS

Your airline will give you customs forms to fill out during your flight regarding the amount of your purchases. Each traveler is allowed to bring in $400 worth of purchases duty-free. Bona fide antiques, works of art, and books are also duty-free. You will be charged 10 percent duty on the next $1,000 worth of purchases, and set customs tariffs on anything over that amount. These tariffs vary, but a beaded or embroidered gown, for example, will carry the top rate of 33 percent. You may want to pick up the brochure "Know Before You Go" from your local customs office, which details customs information for returning residents.

Never try to fool a U.S. Customs officer. If he pulls you aside to inspect your luggage you can be sure that he'll recognize your new Ungaro gown even without the label, and he knows the difference between an art deco knickknack and a bona fide antique. (In case you don't, a true antique must be at least 100 years old, with the papers to prove it.)

CALCULATING YOUR COSTS

Always carry your calculator to determine how much you're paying in dollars. When the exchange rate is an unknown, let the daily rate posted in the banks be your guide. Don't forget to consider any détaxe refund, U.S. Customs duty, and shipping costs in your grand total.

Size Chart

WOMEN'S CLOTHING

American	4	6	8	10	12	14
French	36	38	40	42	44	46
British	8	10	11	12	13	16

WOMEN'S SHOES

American	5	6	7	8	9	10
French	36	37	38	39	40	41
British	3½	4½	5½	6½	7½	8½

BABY CLOTHING

French — Sized to the age of the child. 1m to 18m, "m" meaning months.

CHILDREN'S CLOTHING

French — Sized to the age of the child. 2a to 16a, "a" meaning *ans*, or years.

MEN'S SUITS

American	34	36	38	40	42	44	46	48
French	44	46	48	50	52	54	56	58
British	34	36	38	40	42	44	46	48

MEN'S SHIRTS

American	14	14½	14	15½	16	16½	17	17½	18
French	36	37	38	39	41	42	43	44	45
British	14	14½	14	15½	16	16½	17	17½	18

MEN'S SHOES

American	7	8	9	10	11	12	13
French	39½	41	42	43	44½	46	47
British							

MEN'S HATS

American	6⅞	7⅛	7¼	7⅜	7½
French	55	56	58	59	60
British	6¼	6⅞	7⅛	7¼	7⅜

THE COUTURE

In recent years the cost of *haute couture* clothing, the kind that is miraculously and painstakingly constructed to mold to the body of a private client, has become so high that only an estimated 2,500 women in the world are able to make the glamorous shows and required fittings a part of their lifestyle, and the "death of the *haute couture*" is a hot topic in fashion circles. The French government has even appointed a special committee to bring more relevance to the formidable *Chambre Syndicale de la Haute Couture* by redefining its rules for membership. Happily, for the rest of us, the extravagant collections continue, for their best ideas are distilled into the more moderately priced and often more wearable *prêt-à-porter* (ready-to-wear) collections by the same designers.

Designers put on dazzling shows to debut their collections twice a year for store buyers, the fashion press, and their best customers. While these shows are restricted, in the following weeks you should be able to attend a live or video version of the same in the individual designer's boutiques. For this you must call ahead to reserve, or have your concierge do so.

ALTERATIONS

The better clothing shops will try to accommodate the traveler with fast *retouches* (alterations). I let the shop alter whenever possible because of the very high dressmaking standards and often reasonable prices. Many will deliver altered merchandise to your hotel, *gratis*.

RETURNS

Returns are not generally accepted.

How to Use This Book

MAPS

The numbers on the main shopping district maps (The Left Bank, The Right Bank, The Marais, and The Sixteenth) are a suggested itinerary that can be helpful even if you don't plan to visit every shop. If the shop has more than one location listed, the first address is the most highly recommended and will be numbered on the map.

ADDRESS

A Parisian street address is followed by the *arrondisse-ment* number. Paris is divided into 20 *arrondissements* (districts), arranged numerically in a spiral outward, beginning with the first around the Louvre. In this book, all addresses are followed by the *arrondissement* number. For example, 5th indicates the address is located in the 5th *arrondissement*.

MÉTRO

If you're within walking distance of the shop, this is often the fastest way to get there. The closest métro stop is included in the shop description.

PHONE AND FAX

When you are calling or faxing from the United States, use the country code for France (33), and city code for Paris (1). If you are calling from within Paris, the code (01) must begin every phone number.

OPEN

Store hours change seasonally at many establishments, and most will close for part of August. You (or your concierge) can readily verify open hours by phone.

PRICE RANGE

The range is from inexpensive ($) to very expensive ($$$$).

CREDIT CARDS

The following abbreviations are used for credit cards in this book:
V: Visa, known as Carte Bleue or CB in France
AE: American Express
MC: Master Card, known as Eurocarte or EC in France
DC: Diner's Club

SHOP TALK

Many of the larger shops have some staff that speak English, while at smaller shops this is not necessarily the case. Keep in mind that every shop wants your business and will do its best to understand what you want.

A glossary of French words and phrases not commonly understood by English-speaking foreigners is included on page 175.

The Paris Shopping Companion

Paris Overview

17th

Right Bank

8th

Av. des Champs Elysées

Left B

16th

7th

6t

15th

14th

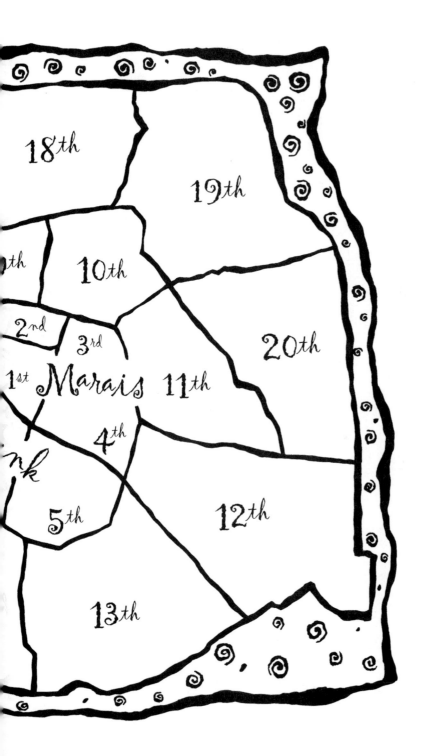

Rive Gauche

The Left Bank, or *Rive Gauche*, is the spiritual home to any student who has ever come to Paris to study at the *Sorbonne* or *Ecole des Beaux-Arts*, and to anyone who has imagined herself in a cafe sipping wine with Jean-Paul Sartre.

The intellectual tradition that began here in 1215 with the establishment of the University, continues in this area known as the *Quartier Latin* (Latin Quarter) since that time when Latin was the tongue of scholars. As you make your way down the Boulevard St-Michel, enjoy the international student milieu, but don't expect to be tempted to do much shopping.

Next door in the Faubourg St-Germain, many venerable French families live in fine old family homes. Here the lifestyle is quiet and understated among those who have nothing to prove, while their centuries' worth of prized but oft-traded possessions stimulate a vibrant antique business throughout the *quartier*.

In these refined surroundings you will find publishing houses, new and old art, meters of fabrics for recovering those inherited pieces of furniture, and the sorts of clothes and accessories that suit a people to whom personal style comes naturally. Somewhere between the conservative and the *avant-garde*, you'll find some of the most interesting shops in the city.

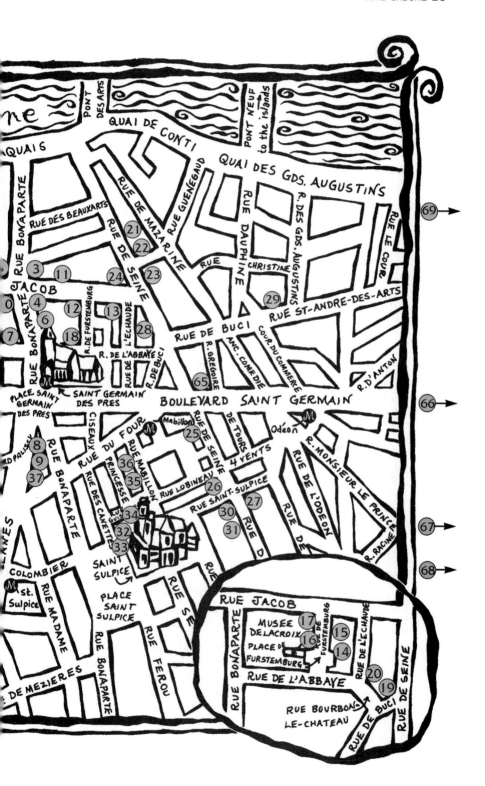

Where To Stay

HOTEL DUC DE SAINT-SIMON

ADDRESS
14 Rue de Saint-Simon, 7th
TELEPHONE
01.45.48.35.66
FAX
01.45.48.68.25
METRO
Rue du Bac
Double rooms from 1000F;
Breakfast 70F
NO CREDIT CARDS

A quiet refuge off St-Germain, this lovely hotel is on one of the most beautiful old streets in Paris. You won't find quarters more gracious than at the Saint-Simon. Every corner exudes sophisticated French charm, and so does the front desk (the very attentive owners happen to be Swedish). Fine antiques, lots of light, an abundance of fresh flowers, and cozy cotton prints make this ambiance unforgettable. The Italian architect Gae Aulenti chose to live here when she was designing the nearby *Musée d'Orsay*. Make your reservations early because word of this hotel is spreading. Just down the block is the restaurant *L'Oeillade* where you can have an outstanding meal for 158F/full dinner, before you retreat to the hotel bar.

HOTEL D'AUBUSSON

ADDRESS
33 Rue Dauphine, 6th
TELEPHONE
01.43.29.43.43
FAX
01.43.29.12.62
METRO
Pont-Neuf
Double rooms from 850F;
Breakfast 80F
CREDIT CARDS
V, MC, AE

The massive oak doors at this historic address open to a 17th century townhouse whose beamed ceilings and Aubusson tapestries speak in the present, offering every comfort. Thanks to a masterful decor by designer Jaques Granges, the warmth of the beautifully appointed public rooms extends to the guest rooms. Sip an *apéritif* at the *Café Laurent*, site of the first literary café in Paris, or take your tea in front of the lobby's Burgundian stone fireplace. You'll feel very much at home in Paris while staying here. Families can be accommodated in the pavilion wing.

HOTEL LE SAINT-GREGOIRE

ADDRESS
43 Rue de l'Abbé-Grégoire, 6th
TELEPHONE
01. 45.48.23.23
FAX
01.45.58.33.95
METRO
St-Placide or Rennes
Double rooms from 650F;
Breakfast 55F

This stylish hotel is extremely popular with French, American, and English guests who appreciate the elegant decor by David Hicks, and great attention to comfort. On a winter's afternoon you'll find them around the roaring lobby fireplace toting shopping bags from the smart boutiques nearby. During summer, the sixth-floor rooms are in demand for their air conditioning, and so is the first-floor double, which has a terrace.

CREDIT CARDS
V, AE, MC

HOTEL DES GRANDES ECOLES

A first-choice hotel for left bankers on a budget, you will find your fellow guests are here to speak at the *Sorbonne*, to show Paris to their children, or are simply saving their money for shopping. A short uphill climb from the métro, this refuge is situated off the street in the midst of a small park. You feel the quiet and calm of the countryside as you take your tea on the terrace overlooking trees and flowers. The sunny breakfast room with lace-covered tables is full of guests who return every year. And at these prices, why not?

ADDRESS
75 Rue du Cardinal Lemoine, 5th
TELEPHONE
01.43.26.79.23
FAX
01.43.25.28.15
METRO
Cardinal Lemoine or Monge
Double rooms from 450F (less without bath); Breakfast 30F
CREDIT CARDS
V, MC

Culture Along the Way

LUXEMBOURG GARDENS

This superb 60-acre garden created by Marie de Médicis is a place of romantic beauty, whose flowered pathways are designed around fountains, sculptures, and ponds, and whose pony rides and marionette theater provide entertainment for the children. Gates open at 9 and close at sunset.

METRO
Luxembourg

MUSÉE D'ORSAY

The Orsay Museum is a masterful transformation from a train station, and the magnificent architecture by Gae Aulenti is nearly as celebrated as its famous impressionist collection. Works from the late 19th and early 20th centuries are elegantly displayed. At the rooftop café you can sit next to murals by Toulouse-Lautrec and view the white domes of *Sacré-Coeur* in the

ADDRESS
1 Rue Bellechasse, 7th
METRO
Solférino

distance. Open 9AM to 6PM during summer and
Sundays year-round; 10AM to 6PM during winter; until
9:45 Thursday nights. Closed Mondays.

MUSEE DE CLUNY

ADDRESS
6 Place Paul Painlevé, 5th
METRO
Cluny

Built by the abbots of Cluny in 1330, the collection of
medieval art housed here includes the Lady and the
Unicorn tapestries in the dazzling mansion adjoining
ancient Roman baths. Open 9:30AM to 5:15PM (closed
12:30 to 2PM during winter), Mon & Wed-Sun.

MUSEE RODIN

ADDRESS
77 Rue de Varenne, 7th
METRO
Varenne

Many of Rodin's best-known works are set in a large
garden surrounding the building where he lived and
worked. *The Thinker* (the original, of course) sits in the
garden above Rodin's tomb. Open 10AM to 5PM, Mon
& Wed-Sun.

Left Bank Shops

1. CARRÉ RIVE GAUCHE
Antique shops

ADDRESS
Area bordered by the Quai
Voltaire, Rue des Sts-Pères, Rue
de l'Université and Rue de Bac
METRO
St-Germain-des-Prés
OPEN
Hours vary
CREDIT CARDS
Accepted by some dealers
$$-$$$$

A delightful way to get to know a favorite part of Paris
is to explore the old, the beautiful, and the curious in
the antique shops of the *Carré Rive Gauche*, an associa-
tion of neighborhood antique dealers. You will find
anything and everything of quality in these shops,
from the grand to the rustic, and you will delight in
the discovery of dealers who are both knowledgeable
and courteous.

The ambiance and antiques continue down the Rue
Jacob and Rue de Seine. Among the most prestigious
names are MADELEINE CASTAIGNE at 21 Rue
Bonaparte, the doyenne of the mixed-period interior,

with rooms running on like stage sets; COMOGLIO at 22 Rue Jacob, a traditional source for set designers and antique reproduction fabrics; and GALERIE CAMOIN at 9 Quai Voltaire, with its magnificently stylish arrangements. Smaller shops filled with fascinating objects for the home are found at every turn.

Sennelier

2. SENNELIER
Art supplies

Chemist Gustave Sennelier opened the family firm in 1887 when he invented a revolutionary type of pastel crayon, now available in over 500 colors and sold throughout the world, and the Senneliers continue to create new products and colors. Van Gogh shopped here, as did Picasso. Celebrated and aspiring artists from Paris and around the world know Sennelier for its history as well as its complete selection of supplies and colors *extraordinaire*.

Located next to the ECOLE DES BEAUX-ARTS, just a glance across the Seine to the Louvre, the store looks much the same as it did 100 years ago, its wooden shelves jammed to accommodate the most modern materials alongside the traditional. Upstairs with graphic and technical supplies you'll find wooden easels made by another branch of the family.

Certainly no artist should miss this store, and I can't think of a more inspiring gift for the young painter than a giant pastel crayon in a brilliant Sennelier color (61F).

ADDRESS
3 Quai Voltaire, 7th
TELEPHONE
01.42.60.72.15
FAX
01.42.61.00.69
METRO
Rue du Bac
OPEN
9AM to noon & 2 to 6PM, Mon;
9AM to 6:15PM, Tue-Sat
CREDIT CARDS
V, AE
$$

ADDRESS
21 Rue Bonaparte, 6th
TELEPHONE
01.44.07.15.99
METRO
St-Germain-des-Prés
OPEN
10AM to 6PM, Mon-Fri; 12 to
7PM Sat
CREDIT CARDS
V, AE, MC
$$$$

3. VICKY TIEL
Women's evening wear

Here you'll discover a ravishing collection of ball-gowns, cocktail dresses, evening suits and wedding gowns tucked into a flower-filled courtyard in one of the oldest buildings in Paris. And you're not the first. The Hollywood crowd has been coming here since American Vicky Tiel established herself in Paris in the 1960s with the help of Elizabeth Taylor.

Glamour has its price, beginning here at 6,000F, but also its standards. The team of seamstresses on the premises are rarely idle, fashioning voluptuously draped frocks from silk, chiffon, wool, taffeta, and beads for women both French and non-French, who have a special understanding of what it is to be "dressed" for an evening.

ADDRESS
23 Rue Bonaparte, 6th (Bed
and cushions)
TELEPHONE
01.43.54.90.73

ADDRESS
25 Rue Bonaparte, 6th (Table)
TELEPHONE
01.46.33.98.71
OPEN
10AM to 7PM, Mon-Sat
CREDIT CARDS
V, AE
$$

4. SIMRANE
Fabrics and household linens

These cottons and silks, hand-printed in Rajasthan, India, are beautifully colored and neatly made into bed and table linens, and include the legendary indigos that are particularly smart at the moment.

In the entrance at the corner of Rue Jacob you'll find an array of rich raw silks to transform your bed or sofa into a voluptuous reception area. Next door are table sets and the like. You can pick up a quilted place mat and matching napkin that will add a cheerful yet exotic touch to your breakfast nook for 100F.

5. TAPISSERIES ROBERT FOUR
Tapestry arts

If you have an interest in tapestry, this is a great place to come for a quick education. Two demonstration looms are in the window: one worked by a weaver, the other by a restorer, neither job a small feat.

Robert Four owns one of Aubusson's ancient tapestry workshops and continues its tradition of vertical method tapestry, training its own weavers. There are only a handful of such restorers in France, qualified by three years of courses and a long practicum. So if you bring Grand-Aunt Clotilde's hunt hanging here for a touch-up, it will be in the most nimble of hands and well worth the hefty fee, as new tapestries start at 60,000F.

Both new and old are available here as well as small cushions with antique tapestry insets beginning at 1,999F—about one-third the cost of new and in mint condition.

ADDRESS
28 Rue Bonaparte and 34 Rue Jacob, 6th (angle)
TELEPHONE
01.43.29.30.60
FAX
01.43.25.33.95
METRO
St-Germain-des-Prés
OPEN
10AM to 7PM, Tue-Fri; 1 to 7PM, Mon
CREDIT CARDS
V, AE
$$$-$$$$

6. FABRICE
Costume jewelry (N.33)
Home accessories (N.54)

Fabrice makes all its own jewelry, to the raves of French fashion writers. This luxury boutique shows styles from the avant-garde to retro to ancient Greece, globetrotting through time for inspiration. A colored lucite ring and wide rounded bracelet inset with colorful fake gems may lie next to an African necklace of large exotic wood beads and another of verdigris that's built like armor.

This intriguing mixture of material and design is very exciting to the Parisian customer, who is undaunted by the choice and has a knack for putting it together. If you buy (pieces start at about 400F), you may assume that confidence too!

Down the street is a striking assortment of home decor pieces, of the new sort designed to look like your grandmother's. While not much is small or sturdy enough to carry home, it is certainly worth a look. You'll find a large collection of vases both rustic and romantic, some with their own ceramic flowers.

ADDRESS
33 & 54 Rue Bonaparte, 6th
TELEPHONE
01.43.26.09.49
METRO
St-Germain-des-Prés
OPEN
10AM to 7PM, Mon-Sat
CREDIT CARDS
V, AE
$$$

ADDRESS
40 Rue Bonaparte, 6th
(Furniture)
38 Rue Bonaparte, 6th (Fabrics
and wallpaper)
TELEPHONE
01.43.29.21.50
FAX
01.43.29.77.57
METRO
St-Germain-des-Prés
OPEN
9:30AM to 6:30PM, Mon-Sat;
closed one week in August
CREDIT CARDS
V, AE, DC
$$$

7. NOBILIS
Interior decoration and luggage

It is only fitting that so many of the city's most beautiful interiors stores make their home in one of Paris's most refined neighborhoods. Nobilis has brought fine fabrics to the discerning fingertips of the *haute bourgeoisie* since 1928. Here is where they come to choose coverings for their most noble pieces of furniture and the walls of their period apartments, and you may too.

If your taste runs to glass and steel, you will be pleased to know that Nobilis has added contemporary choices to its classic damasks and *chinoiserie* prints. Choose a Napoleonic-style chair in the shop at N.40, and its upholstery at N.38. Carry them home, since Nobilis won't ship. Whether you come to buy or browse, you won't feel lost or unwelcome as you flip through the fabric boards.

ADDRESS
54 Rue Bonaparte, 6th
TELEPHONE
01.43.26.84.11
METRO
St-Germain-des-Prés

ADDRESS
273 Rue St- Honoré, 8th
TELEPHONE
01.42.61.41.14
METRO
Concorde

ADDRESS
23 Avenue Victor Hugo, 16th
TELEPHONE
01.45.00.83.19
METRO
Etoile
OPEN
11AM to 7PM, Mon; 10 to 7PM,
Tue-Sat
CREDIT CARDS
V, AE, MC, DC
$$-$$$

8. GEORGE RECH
Women's clothing

Rech is a smart stop for anyone looking for discreetly cut pants or skirts, jackets or coat. His separates are cited as among the best in Paris by the French fashion press, but you'd never know it without a close look. Clothes that seem to hang straight on the rack take a shape of their own when you step into them, even if you're not French. There's something to flatter every figure, each in a dozen or so fabrics. While these classics come well priced in his *Synonyme* line, the George Rech line is trendier and pricier.

Along the Way

The church ST-GERMAIN-DES-PRÉS is the oldest in Paris. The tower and belfry have stood since the 10th century and are now surrounded by Romanesque additions. At its zenith, when its riches and allegiance belonged to the pope, the church rivaled the city of Paris in power.

Today it is known for evening concerts of classical music and a garden statue given by Picasso in tribute to his poet friend Apollinaire. Entering the glass doors to the sanctuary you'll find relief from the noisy bustle of streetlife on the Boulevard St-Germain. To prolong the calm, explore the more tranquil neighborhood to the north of the boulevard.

9. FRANÇOIS VILLON
Men's and women's shoes

Villon shoes are built for comfort along with that little something that is a subtle twist on the classic. If you prefer to step out sporting a classic pump in a rich fabric or tone, smashing with a matching bag, step in here. The boots are extraordinary leg-hugging fashion.

ADDRESS
58 Rue Bonaparte, 6th
TELEPHONE
01.43.25.98.36
METRO
St-Germain-des-Prés
OPEN
10:30AM to 7PM, Mon-Sat;
closed part of August
CREDIT CARDS
V, AE, MC, DC
$$$

ADDRESS
33 Rue Jacob, 6th
TELEPHONE
01.42.60.80.72
METRO
St-Germain-des-Prés
OPEN
2:30 to 7PM, Mon; 10AM to
7PM, Tue-Sat
CREDIT CARDS
V, AE
$$$

LES OUVRAGES DU PETIT
FAUNE
Sewing Kits Only
ADDRESS
89 Rue de Rennes, 6th
TELEPHONE
01.42-22-63-69
METRO
St-Sulpice
OPEN
10AM to 7PM, Mon-Sat
NO CREDIT CARDS
$

10. PETIT FAUNE
Children's clothing

Very civilized clothing for your little fawn from
infancy to age 6. The small collection is entirely in
cotton, mostly Liberty of London prints, and wool that
is hand-knitted. If a lovely little dress at 390 to 600F
doesn't suit your budget, perhaps you would like to
bring back for her an adorable doll rattle wearing a
smaller version of the same dress and a boating hat in a
matching print for him, each for 120F.

If you're able to do-it-yourself, head directly to the
OUVRAGES DU PETIT FAUNE boutique on the Rue
de Rennes. Here you will find sewing kits for 10 differ-
ent patterns or 5 knitted outfits. A detailed pattern,
including cloth, buttons, and even the PETIT FAUNE
label will cost you about one-third of the completed
garment on the Rue Jacob.

ADDRESS
26 Rue Jacob, 6th
TELEPHONE
01.43.25.67.00
METRO
St-Germain-des-Prés
OPEN
10AM to 7PM, Mon-Sat
CREDIT CARDS
V, AE
$$

11. LA MAISON RUSTIQUE
Books and T-shirts

If you are interested in French style but only read pictures in French, this is a bookstore for you. The publisher Flammarion has built an attractive shop in the
guise of a rustic refuge for its beautifully photographed
titles specializing in interior decoration, gardening,
and nature. While some titles are offered in English,
would an English translation of *The Art of Folding Napkins*
really help?

For the less serious-minded is an elegant collection
of T-shirts from the worlds of 20th-century French art
and literature. A Delaunay, Cocteau, or Magritte is
180F in an adult size or 145F in children's sizes. You
may receive a Flammarion book catalog free of charge
from this address.

12. L'ATELIER D'ANAIS
Needle arts

This comfy store sells old-fashioned but practical needlework tools: bird-shaped scissors with a cutting beak; a thimble topped with a ceramic Scottie dog to take home to Grandma. There are also made-up petit point pillows and hand-painted canvasses with traditional French motifs.

If your shopping partner has little interest in such details, let him settle into one of the flowered needle-point armchairs and pet Madame's obediently mournful doggie while she pulls tassles and threads from the many paisley-covered drawers that line the wall. If you know exactly what you want, the shop will paint a custom canvas for you.

ADDRESS
23 Rue Jacob, 6th
TELEPHONE
01.43.26.68.00
METRO
St-Germain-des-Prés
OPEN
11AM to12 noon & 2 to 6PM,
Tue, Fri, Sat
NO CREDIT CARDS
$$

13. A LA BONNE RENOMME
Women's clothing and accessories

Here you'll find that funky gypsy feeling with a French touch. Designers Catherine Legrand and Elisabeth Gratacap piece together fabrics from all around France with heavy embroidered and velvet ribbons that we usually associate with upholstery trims or 18th-century gowns to produce rich patchwork designs in dark tones. Peek into the workshop at the Rue Vieille-du-Temple location to watch seamstresses craft a collection of skirts, vests, cushions, and handbags of all shapes and sizes, hats, coats, and quilts, none like another and the whole like nothing else you'll ever see.

This may not be your look head to toe, but if you suspect there's a little gypsy in you, try a tassled earring or a turban or another of the sensationally shaped hats. There are lots of little gifts here, beginning with decorative key rings at 90F, coin purses, and hair ornaments. The very popular and colorful purses begin at 340F.

ADDRESS
1 Rue Jacob, 6th
TELEPHONE
01.46.33.90.67
METRO
St-Germain-des-Prés
OPEN
11AM to 7PM, Mon-Sat

ADDRESS
26 Rue Vieille-du-Temple, 4th
TELEPHONE
01.42.72.03.86
METRO
St-Paul
OPEN
11AM to 7PM, Mon-Sat
CREDIT CARDS
V
$$-$$$

Along the Way

The PLACE DE FURSTEMBERG is one of the most charming in Paris, and a frequent location for movie scenes and publicity spots, yet it remains hidden from the crowds. Fragrant mauve-blossomed trees carry perfume across the way to the tiny DELACROIX MUSEUM, 6 Rue de Furstemberg, where the great Romantic painter lived and produced his passionate works. On this small street, every shop reflects the local reputation for beauty.

Place de Furstemberg

ADDRESS
7 Place de Furstemberg, 6th
TELEPHONE
01.43.25.75.98
METRO
St-Germain-des-Prés
OPEN
10AM to 7PM, Mon-Sat; closed one week in August
NO CREDIT CARDS
$$$

14. MANUEL CANOVAS
Fabrics and wallpapers showroom

When Canovas opened his very exclusive decorator fabric showroom to the public, the interior design world of Paris was up in arms over this unheard-of practice. After all, Canovas was one of the city's top decorators as well as textile designers.

Now his upholstery fabrics and wall coverings, the height of Parisian chic, are available direct from this location at prices substantially lower than your decorator will charge you through his U.S. showroom; however, you must arrange your own shipping. For lower prices still, look here and buy from Coolman.

15. MANUEL CANOVAS BOUTIQUE
Household linens and fragrances, shawls, beachwear

Enter through M. Canovas's private garden. Inside this enormously appealing boutique you will find his collection for bed and table in cheery florals or simple geometrics, available here alone. You will be tempted to turn your bedroom into a pretty boudoir, and why not? Choose a fresh bouqueted duvet and sheets (American sizes can be made up in 10 days) with ruffled cases, a kimono and nightgown in a matching cotton print. Add the heaven-scented candle in a frosted glass that burns for 45 hours, and nothing will be the same. A popular gift, the candle comes beautifully boxed and wrapped for 230F.

Also important sellers are the exquisite shawls—enveloping 4.5-foot squares of cashmere or silk that say it all for 3,000 to 4,000F. If you are considering a warmer climate, don't miss the equally distinctive beach collection. A one-piece suit, sarong, and bag may be just what you need for those excursions between the juice bar and resort pool. Of the two locations, the original at Place de Furstemberg is the more charming.

ADDRESS
5 Place de Furstemberg, 6th
TELEPHONE
01.43.26.89.31
METRO
St-Germain-des-Prés
OPEN
10AM to 7PM, Mon-Sat

ADDRESS
30 Avenue Georges V, 8th
TELEPHONE
01.49.52.00.36
METRO
Georges V
OPEN
10AM to 7PM, Mon-Sat
CREDIT CARDS
V, AE
$$$

Manuel Canovas

ADDRESS
4 Rue Furstemberg, 6th
TELEPHONE
01.43.26.56.91
METRO
St-Germain-des-Prés
OPEN
11AM to 7PM, Mon-Fri; Sat
afternoons; closed August
NO CREDIT CARDS
$$$

16. YVELINE
Antiques

Yveline has an eye for the unusual that will delight the jaded antique hunter. In this lovely shop where allegiance is to distinction rather than to a specific period, you may find that fascinating dining set, a 19th-century still life, or wonderful wooden hands for the sofa table. The gracefully articulated hands were once artist's models and are a specialty here, selling in the range of 2,000F per pair. With 36 years' involvement ir antiques everything Yveline chooses is quite special.

Along the Way

The MARCHE BIOLOGIQUE (organic market), on the Boulevard Raspail between the Rue de Cherche-Midi and the Rue de Rennes, is where *tout Paris* comes to do its weekly organic marketing. On Sunday mornings from 9AM to 1PM, vendors are open for business, drawing health and quality-conscious Parisians to their open-air stands for wonderful jams and honeys, savory buckwheat galettes (pancakes) filled with vegetables and cheese to consume on the spot, and creamy unpasteurized goat cheeses that you can take back to your hotel but not back to the U.S. This large and popular market becomes increasingly crowded as the morning wears on, so it's best to go early.

ADDRESS
7 Rue Jacob, 6th
TELEPHONE
01.43.26.82.61
METRO
St-Germain-des-Prés

ADDRESS
22 Rue Royale, 8th
TELEPHONE
01.49.26.04.77
METRO
Madeleine

17. PIERRE FREY
Home accessories

Patrick Frey carries on the tradition of his father, Pierre Frey, Parisian decorator par excellence. He has a wonderful way with textile creations fashioned from Frey signature fabrics into welted pillows (from 360F), cashmere throws (1,500F), handbags and luggage, table covers and bedroom linens, and smaller well-priced gifty items. The looks run from 18th-century style to freshly colored plaids.

Pierre Frey

ADDRESS
47 Rue des Petits-Champs, 1st
TELEPHONE
01.44.77.36.00
METRO
Pyramides
OPEN
10AM to 7PM, Mon-Sat
CREDIT CARDS
V, AE
$$$

18. LA REUNION DES MUSÉES NATIONAUX
Art posters

Don't leave Paris without an impressionist poster for your guest bath. This state-run shop has handled posters printed for exhibitions in the 34 national museums of France since 1970. Posters from permanent collections are 45F, and those from special exhibitions are 35F. They also publish and sell a few books on the national museums, such as the amusing *Versailles ABC* for the child becoming culturally fluent by recognizing an angel, balcony, and carriage in the Louis XIV style, and reading them in French. Note that this shop remains open on Tuesdays when most museum shops are closed.

ADDRESS
10 Rue de L'Abbaye, 6th
TELEPHONE
01.43.29.21.45
FAX
01.43.29.66.53
METRO
St-Germain-des-Prés
OPEN
10AM to 6:30PM, Mon-Fri
CREDIT CARDS
V
$

ADDRESS
1 & 2 Rue du Bourbon-Le-
Château, 6th
TELEPHONE
01.43.26.40.23
METRO
St-Germain-des-Prés
OPEN
10:30AM to 7:15PM, Tue-Sat;
closed August
CREDIT CARDS
V, MC
$$-$$$

19. FRANÇOISE THIBAULT

Home accessories

This boutique that Mme Thibault has tended and per-
fected for over 30 years exudes a particularly great
French charm, as does Madame. At first glance it
appears to house antiques, but a closer look reveals
beautiful objects recently handcrafted in France and
around Europe. The boxes painted with cats or a village scene may be from Russia or Germany, but here
they look French.

You're on your own when it comes to shipping
from her extraordinary collection of flowered chandeliers with crystal drops, framed mirrors, and painted
furniture, but as you meander through the nooks and
crannies of this shop, you will certainly find decorative
knickknacks you will want to tuck into your suitcase
and carry home.

Françoise Thibault

20. SALLE À MANGER
Vintage porcelaines, ceramics, and crystal

With the current fad for vintage tablewear, hosts and hostesses are beating a path to the door of Michel Pepé's small shop, where the patterns move in and out with the blink of an eye. M. Pepé strives to bring his clientele complete sets of dishes, dating from the late 19th-century through the 1950s.

A 135-piece set of 1940s Haviland china in top condition was spotted here at a fraction of what it would be sold at new. Another favored specialty is pieces from the Vallauris region, where Picasso worked in clay, drawing a coterie of artists who made the area a ceramics center in the '50s. Feel free to go to town here, as M. Pepé will take care of your shipping arrangements.

ADDRESS
4 Rue de Bourbon-Le-Château, 6th
TELEPHONE
01.40.46.91.42
METRO
St-Germain-des-Prés
OPEN
2:30 to 7PM, Mon; 10AM to 7PM, Tue-Sat; often Sun afternoons
CREDIT CARDS
V, AE, MC
$$-$$$

Along the Way

The OPEN AIR FOOD MARKET beginning at St-Germain and running down the Rue de Seine and Rue de Buci, is one of the most picturesque in Paris. In the early hours the merchants begin arriving to arrange their stands with an artist's eye for color, shape and texture, so for shame if you touch the merchandise! From 9AM to 1PM and 4 to 7PM, Tues-Sat, and on Sunday mornings, the streets are jammed with Parisians doing their daily marketing. This time-honored tradition has the makings of a terrific picnic.

☕ LA PALETTE
Café

ADDRESS
43 Rue de Seine, 6th
TELEPHONE
01.43.26.68.15
METRO
Mabillon
OPEN
8AM to 2AM, Mon-Sat; hot meals served noon to 3PM
NO CARDS
$

La Palette was a favorite hang-out of mine during student days, and nothing here has changed. Forever a neighborhood café filled with a lively mix of students, artists, dealers, and their patrons, you'll find the outdoor tables crowded whenever there's some sun, and the inside full of chatter. Baguette sandwiches, delectable fruit tarts, and the flavor of this artsy quarter are available all day.

Rue de Buci Open Air Food Market

ADDRESS
51 Rue de Seine, 6th
TELEPHONE
01.43.54.57.65
METRO
St-Germain-des-Prés
OPEN
11AM to noon & 2 to 6:30PM,
Tue-Sat
CREDIT CARDS
V, AE
$$-$$$$

21. JACQUELINE SUBRA
Antique jewelry

Don't hesitate to buzz open this gem of a shop. Jacqueline and her daughter will invite you to admire their collection of the real thing in jewelry from the late 1800s through the 1960s, much of which now inspires fashionable fakes. Their selections over the past quarter-century, from the coffers of families with taste but diminishing means and from dealers who know of their reputation, represent the finest examples from each stylistic period. But don't worry, Madame assures me that there is always a selection at 700F for little gifts.

22. GALERIE DOCUMENTS
Original posters

I hope that proprietor Mireille Romand is in when you come to call. As great-great-granddaughter of the founder of this institution, she will be able to tell you (in English) everything about the vast domain of original posters in her remarkable collection. Her ancestor, a print dealer, began collecting posters when they were just being invented and this shop was the first in the world to sell them. All are from the early days of lithographic posters (about 1870 to 1950), which explains their superb color.

Choose from the 1,000 or so posters announcing air and motor expositions, theatrical events, interesting inventions and more, each with historic and artistic value and reliable documentation. If you're not set on a Toulouse-Lautrec, which you can also find here, you may pick up something wonderful for 800F.

ADDRESS
53 Rue de Seine, 6th
TELEPHONE
01.43.54.50.68
METRO
St-Germain-des-Près
OPEN
2 to 7PM, Mon; 10:30AM to 7PM, Tue-Sat
CREDIT CARDS
V, AE
$$-$$$$

Rue de Seine

23. GALERIE JEANNE-BUCHER
Art gallery

ADDRESS
53 Rue de Seine, 6th (Inside courtyard)
TELEPHONE
01.43.26.22.32
FAX
01.43.29.47.04
METRO
St-Germain-des-Prés
OPEN
9AM to 1PM & 2 to 6:30PM, Tues-Fri; 10AM to noon & 2:30 to 6:30PM, Sat
CREDIT CARDS
V
$$$-$$$$

This highly respected art gallery has proven an uncanny ability to recognize important new art since its beginnings in 1925. The cubists and surrealists were shown here early on, and gallery director Jean-François Jaeger can probably still pull a Miro, Picasso, or Dubuffet from his vaults for the serious buyer. His current stable of international artists has its future in good hands.

24. MIMI LA SARDINE
Women's clothing

ADDRESS
54 Rue de Seine, 6th
TELEPHONE
01.46.34.11.66
METRO
Mabillon or Odéon
OPEN
2 to 7:30PM, Mon; 10AM to 7:30PM, Tue-Sat
CREDIT CARDS
V, AE, MC
$$

You don't really have to be built like a sardine to look good in this comfortable collection of sporty coordinates entirely in vibrant cotton velours. Mostly solids in about 30 colors and mix and match shapes, the pieces are designed for all seasons.

Pick up a Spencer jacket and miniskirt, or pants, topcoat, vest, cardigan, and culotte, and top off the look with a beret or headband. The concept is American but the look and shape are definitely French.

25. GERARD MULOT
Bakery

ADDRESS
76 Rue de Seine, 6th
TELEPHONE
01.46.33.49.27
METRO
Mabillon
OPEN
6:45AM to 8PM, Thurs-Tues
NO CREDIT CARDS
$$

This attractive neighborhood bakery is always crowded with locals in the know. They come for the tempting pastries, *pain aux noix* (walnut bread), and fresh chocolates in bright red boxes. If you're a macaroon fan, don't miss these!

26. SOULEIADO
Fabrics, wallpapers, home accessories, clothing

ADDRESS
78 Rue de Seine, 6th
TELEPHONE
01.43.54.15.13
METRO
Odéon
OPEN
10AM to 7PM, Mon-Sat
CREDIT CARDS
V, AE, MC, DC
$$$

You may already know this enchanting store by its American name, Pierre Deux. This is the authentic version of the well-loved French provincial print.

It all began when Charles Démery, a native of Provence, found 40,000 wooden fabric-printing plates from the 18th and 19th centuries in his uncle's barn. The enterprise he created in 1938, to produce textiles from traditional provincial fabrics by the old methods, has succeeded by the highest standard. M. Demery has modernized and popularized this ancient art of his region, and his fabrics are recognized and appreciated well outside of France.

This shop glows with the warmth of the sun, colors, and lifestyle of Provence. The original motifs have been modernized by enlarging or diminishing them, mixing them, and reproducing them in rich tones. Choose to join the ranks of those seduced by Souleiado, and you, too, will re-cover your sofas and chairs, wallpaper your bedroom, throw a new quilt on the bed and linens on the table, strew lavender sachets throughout your home, and put everything from Kleenex to hats in print-covered boxes. Then revitalize your wardrobe with shawls and folklorique skirts. Start with a sachet at 16F, or a black lacy skirt at 1,000F.

Fabrics (enter next door) cannot be shipped by the shop to the U.S., but as all else, they are cheaper here than in the States. For another version of the look at more moderate prices, step across the street into LES OLIVADES.

ADDRESS
1 Rue de Tournon, 6th
TELEPHONE
01.43.54.14.54
METRO
Mabillon
OPEN
10AM to 7PM, Mon-Sat
CREDIT CARDS
V, AE, MC
$$-$$$

27. LES OLIVADES
Fabrics, home accessories, clothing

This tiny bit of Provence is full of everything made from the traditional warm prints of southern France. A lesser-known (at least to foreigners) producer of provencial textiles than Pierre Deux (known as SOULEIDO in France, and just across the street) Les Olivades has the cachet of an older and less commercial operation with a less expensive product. Yardage prices begin at 110F per meter, and there are plenty of made-up items.

ADDRESS
6 Rue de L'Echaudé, 6th
TELEPHONE
01.46.33.88.88
FAX
01.43.29.74.28
METRO
Mabillon or St-Germain-des-Prés
OPEN
2:30 to 7:30PM, Mon; 10AM to 7:30PM, Tues-Sat
CREDIT CARDS
V, AE
$$

28. PIXI & CIE
Collectibles

To see the French as they see themselves, stop in at Pixi, a miniature world of hand-painted lead figures that begins with the toy soldier, and extends to charming representations of Parisian life. Look closely at the nanny, the red-cheeked policeman, the baker and his baguettes, and the well-turned-out golfer all teed up or the jazzman at his horn.

If you have runway taste, this *haute couture* collection is a must. Wonderfully executed figurines modeling the finest French couture fashions of the century are presented, each in her own small box that stands open for display with a reflection strip for viewing the handsomely painted garments from all sides, complete with the designer's logo opposite. If you've always wanted a Worth creation or a '60s St. Laurent, you'll find it here in the 165F version.

For the young and hip are scenes with Tin-Tin, and other comic strip heros. You'll also find here a sought-after collection of Tin-Tin T-shirts, and lots of inexpensive knickknacks with plenty of gift potential.

☕ LA ROTISSERIE D'EN FACE

Restaurant

ADDRESS
2 Rue Christine, 6th
TELEPHONE
01.43.26.40.98
METRO
St-Michel or Odéon
OPEN
12:30 to 2PM & 7 to 10PM, Mon-Fri; 7 to 10PM, Sat; closed August
CREDIT CARDS
V, AE, MC, DC

Light and appealing in both ambiance and cuisine, star chef Jacques Cagna's homey bistro draws a smart crowd, and is a favorite among Americans. They come here for its spit-roasted entrées, imaginative daily specials, and luscious desserts. The menu is from 135F at lunch and 198F at dinner. Reservations are a must.

29. MARIANNE GRAY

Beauty salon

ADDRESS
52 Rue St-André-des-Arts, 6th
TELEPHONE
01.43.26.58.21
METRO
Odéon or St-Michel
OPEN
10AM to 6PM, Mon-Sat; Fri evenings
CREDIT CARDS
V, MC
$$

Not for the Glamour Cat! The ancient stone interior, tiled floor, and beamed ceilings of this 18th-century building bespeak a respect for the natural that extends from the stylist to your coiffure. No rushed jobs or copycat dos, and no harsh products are to be found.

As you sit wrapped in a French provincial robe, studying the reflection of a wall gargoyle in the mirror, today's world drops away. An easy, simple coif is the trademark here, and it draws both the neighborhood and an intellectual movie star clientele who don't want hair abused by frequent changes. Stay for a massage, facial, and manicure, and take home natural hair care products bearing the house label.

ADDRESS
2 Rue de Tournon, 6th
TELEPHONE
01.46.33.41.03
METRO
Odéon
OPEN
10:15AM to 7PM, Mon-Sat

ADDRESS
45 Avenue Victor Hugo, 16th
TELEPHONE
01.45.01.73.00
METRO
Victor Hugo
OPEN
10:15AM to 7PM, Mon-Sat
CREDIT CARDS
V, AE
$$$

ADDRESS
6 Rue Pierre Lescot, 1st (Outlet
store)
METRO
Etienne-Marcel
OPEN
10AM to 6PM, Mon-Sat
NO CREDIT CARDS
$$

30. EMMANUELLE KHANH
Women's clothing

To the French, Emmanuelle Khanh is a classic name for beautifully cut-out necklines, embroideries, and sophisticated eyelet designs. Such refined details are subtly placed to draw attention to the face, the chest, or the thigh. Certainly she is feminine and seductive to the American eye and this is a good address for the beguiling suit, for the sweater with an engaging motif, and for the hand-embroidered silk blouse that originally made her name. The Emmanuelle Khanh wholesale outlet has lots of bargains but no dressing rooms, and credit cards are not accepted.

31. AU NOM DE LA ROSE
Roses

Scented garden roses, with strains dating back to the 17th-century, are freshly cut every day for this irresistible shop. The 60 varieties of roses here are favored by those in the fashion world seeking the perfect shade of bud or bloom (8-15F a stem). Bouquets are beautifully wrapped in white paper tied with a rose, and look terribly Parisian. The Rue du Bac location has a boutique selling rose jam, rose soaps, and other gift possibilities made of roses.

ADDRESS
4 Rue du Tournon, 6th
TELEPHONE
01.46.34.10.64
METRO
Odéon
OPEN
8:30AM to 9PM, Mon-Sat; 10AM to 2PM & 3 to 6PM, Sun

ADDRESS
46 Rue du Bac, 7th
TELEPHONE
01.42.22.08.09
METRO
Rue du Bac
OPEN
9AM to 9PM, Mon-Sat; 9AM to 2PM, Sun (this location closed August)
CREDIT CARDS
V, MC, DC
$$-$$$$

Along the Way

On the PLACE ST-SULPICE, a magnificent church shares space with the towering FOUNTAIN OF THE CARDINAL POINTS, its aura of religious serenity intact. On glorious summer days you may come upon book and antique fairs here, and on July 14, one of the grandest of Bastille Day balls. The boutiques facing the square are equally elegant.

ADDRESS
6 Place St-Sulpice, 6th
(Women's)
TELEPHONE
01.43.29.43.00
METRO
St-Sulpice

ADDRESS
12 Place St-Sulpice, 6th
(Men's)
TELEPHONE
01.43.26.84.40
METRO
St-Sulpice

ADDRESS
38 Rue du Faubourg St-Honoré
(Women's)
TELEPHONE
01.42.65.74.59
METRO
Concorde

ADDRESS
32 Rue du Faubourg St-Honoré
(Shoes and accessories)
TELEPHONE
01.42.65.01.15
METRO
Concorde

ADDRESS
9 Rue de Grenelle, 7th
(Variation line)
TELEPHONE
01.45.44.39.01
METRO
Sèvres-Babylone
OPEN
10AM to 7PM, Mon-Sat
CREDIT CARDS
V, AE
$$$-$$$$

YVES ST-LAURENT COUTURE

ADDRESS
5 Avenue Marçeau, 16th
TELEPHONE
01.44.31.64.00
METRO
Alma-Marçeau

32. YVES ST-LAURENT RIVE GAUCHE
Women's and men's clothing

St-Laurent has been the king of Paris fashion since his first collection for Dior in 1968. If you take this opportunity to purchase his *prêt-à-porter* (ready-to-wear), you'll know some of the reasons why. He has had the genius to introduce collections that kept the fashion world wildly excited, season after season, and his innovations have become classics. The YSL you buy today is elegantly cut and enormously comfortable, and will still be so when you put it on 10 years from now.

St-Laurent was the first designer to open a *prêt-à-porter* boutique, taking the formality and high prices out of fashion found in the rarified couture milieu. The left bank location is his largest, but located out of the tourist hub it's quieter than the others. If YSL is what you want, come here for the quickest and most attentive service and to best view the extensive collection. In the women's boutique downstairs look for suits, dresses, skirts, accessories, and leathers, upstairs for shoes and furs. The Variation line, designed in the style of, but not by, St-Laurent, is lower-priced. The secrets of his *haute couture* (custom-fit clothing) are found only at the boutique on Avenue Marçeau. No sales here.

OPEN
9:30AM to 6:30PM, Mon-Fri
CREDIT CARDS
V, AE
$$$$

33. MARIE MERCIÉ
Women's hats

Hats off to Marie Mercié, who designs headgear with humor, grace, and history. A walk through her boutique is like a whimsical world tour, taking you from Fontainebleau to Africa. Since her first collection in 1985, she has brought contemporary chic to this important Parisian accessory by creating hats that will be noticed for their daring without losing their elegance, winning the hearts and heads of younger French thoroughbreds. If you want to wow them at Ascot, consider the straw adorned with a perfect giant sunflower, marred by a housefly.

There are no limits to shapes, colors, and decorations of her millinery and its loosely coordinating jewelry and handbags. For bridal, go to the Rue Tiquetonne boutique where they customize.

ADDRESS
23 Rue St-Sulpice, 6th
TELEPHONE
01.43.26.45.83
METRO
St-Sulpice
OPEN
10AM to 7PM, Tue-Sat

ADDRESS
56 Rue Tiquetonne, 2nd
(Orders taken)
TELEPHONE
01.40.26.60.68
METRO
Etienne-Marcel
OPEN
10AM to 7PM, Mon-Sat
CREDIT CARDS
V, AE
$$$

ADDRESS
40 Rue St-Sulpice, 6th
TELEPHONE
01.43.26.25.31
METRO
St-Sulpice
OPEN
10AM to 1PM & 2 to 7PM, Tue-
Sat; 2 to 7PM, Mon
CREDIT CARDS
V, AE, MC
$$-$$$

34. BEAUTÉ DIVINE
Antiques and new bath accessories

If you're looking for a very personal gift, or something deco with which to make your toilette, you will be intrigued by Mme Régine de Robien's renowned collection of beauty articles from the early 1900s. Everything for the bath is here at all prices, and in impeccable condition.

For those who forswear the already-used, there's a selection of new items in the spirit of the old, even Madame's line of turn-of-the-century ivory-looking hairbrushes (130F plus 145F and 3 days for engraved initials). She is an expert in perfume bottles, selling twice a year at the Parisian auction house Drouot, and you will find many outstanding examples in the shop, some still filled with their original perfume.

An easy purchase might be a stunning heavily geometric bottle of colored bubble bath (100F); an antique razor (30F), lipstick holder or hatpin; or new fringed toweling on an antique rack. Whatever you choose, you'll leave with lovely smelling perfume grains tucked into every parcel.

ADDRESS
16 Rue Guisarde, 6th
TELEPHONE
01.43.54.32.06
METRO
Mabillon
OPEN
10:30AM to 12:30PM & 1:30 to
7PM, Mon-Sat
CREDIT CARDS
V
$$$

35. AU PLAT D'ETAIN
Toy soldiers

Since before the French Revolution, young Parisians have been coming to this store to admire the first lead soldiers and listen to grownups talk military strategy in the back room. It still draws the serious enthusiast of military metal, dealing in the venerated French makers C. B. G., Mignot, and Lucotte, as well as the English house Tradition.

The battle scene dioramas are spectacular. If you shun combat, look for the beautifully dressed Cyrano de Bergerac sporting a nose almost as long as his sword, or the aristocratic carriage and four, filled with passengers who could be fleeing revolutionary wrath. Soldiers begin at 150F.

36. THE VILLAGE VOICE
Books

Parisian Odile Hellier opened her shop over a decade ago to carry on the American literary tradition in Paris, and a fine literary hangout it has become. You probably won't find the bestsellers here, but you will find two floors of English language books by English-speaking writers the world over. Specialties are new American writing and English translations of contemporary French works.

The Village Voice Readers Series brings a major writer here every month or so for a reading and book signing. There is also a good selection of American magazines.

ADDRESS
6 Rue Princesse, 6th
TELEPHONE
01.46.33.36.47
METRO
Mabillon
OPEN
10AM to 8PM, Tues-Sat; 2 to 8PM, Mon
NO CREDIT CARDS
$$

37. POM D'API
Children's shoes

The multicolor mosaic storefront has tremendous kid appeal among the artfully austere facades of this grown-up city. Inside it's filled with fanciful Pom d'Api label footwear for children to 12 years (to French size 40).

Whether it be bright suede lace-ups, tennies in foreign-looking color combos, or leopard-skin-like booties, these shoes can't fail to please the modern child. Cloth sneakers are from 150F, and leather shoes 400F-700F.

ADDRESS
28 Rue du Four, 6th
TELEPHONE
01.45.48.39.31
METRO
Mabillon
OPEN
10:15AM to 7PM, Mon-Sat

ADDRESS
13 Rue du Jour, 1st
TELEPHONE
01.42.36.08.87
METRO
Les Halles
OPEN
10:30AM to 7PM, Mon-Fri; Sat to 7:30PM

ADDRESS
140 Avenue Victor-Hugo, 16th
TELEPHONE
01.47.27.22.00
METRO
Victor-Hugo
OPEN
2 to 7PM, Mon; 10AM to 7PM, Tue-Sat
CREDIT CARDS
V, AE
$$-$$$

ADDRESS
60 Rue du Cherche Midi, 6th
TELEPHONE
01.45.49.45.96
METRO
Sèvres-Babylone
OPEN
10:30AM to 7PM, Tue-Sat
CREDIT CARDS
V, AE, MC
$$-$$$

38. LES CONTES DE THE
Teas and teapots

Cultivators of teatime will find a treasure-trove here.
More than 100 varieties of tea are sold alongside the
products and accoutrements that complete a perfect
tea service. I come here for the extraordinary selection
of teapots that Mme Dattner has chosen from around
the world. Whether you prefer Russian motifs, reproduction Meissen, or pots in the shape of houses or animals, you'll find them all in this delightful little shop.

ADDRESS
23 Rue du Cherche-Midi, 6th
TELEPHONE
01.45.44.29.40
METRO
St-Sulpice
OPEN
10:30AM to 7PM, Mon-Sat
CREDIT CARDS
V, AE
$$

39. J. B. MARTIN
Women's shoes

This is the first Paris boutique for the large Breton fac-
tory, which has been making shoes for other labels for
years. Because there is no intermediary, these very
wearable shoes are particularly well priced: from 500F,
which is French middle market.

You'll find lots of low-heeled, casual shoes here,
many in soft suedes. If you need a fresh pair of walking
shoes for tomorrow, step right in. But if you're looking
for fancy French footwear, you're best off looking up
and down this block, chock full of boutiques selling
shoes and handbags.

ADDRESS
17 Rue du Cherche-Midi, 6th
TELEPHONE
01.45.44.46.54
METRO
St-Sulpice
OPEN
10:30AM to 7PM, Mon-Sat
CREDIT CARDS
V, AE
$$-$$$

40. SOPHIE D'ANNUNZIA
Lingerie and hosiery

This narrow little shop, crowded with merchandise,
looks like any neighborhood lingerie stop until you go
through the collection. A mother-daughter affair that
specializes in very feminine prewar styles, the distinc-
tive choices reflect a chic nostalgia that avoids a con-
temporary look. Within that glamorous reference,
you'll find the most desirable models from the top
French lines. Bustiers, stockings, negligees, and
swimwear, as well as bras and panties are here at vari-
ous prices.

41. AU CHAT DORMANT
Cat collectibles

This place is the cat's meow if you love to surround yourself with things kitty. You will find cats on postards, paintings, and prints; cat bookends; cat figures of tremendous charm painted on rocks, boxes, and trays, on cushions and pincushions; cat sculptures, even lamps shaped like cats. Nothing feline escapes the notice of the kindly owner of this delightful establishment. And no wonder—she has the eyes of a cat!

ADDRESS
13 Rue du Cherche-Midi, 6th
TELEPHONE
01.45.49.48.63
METRO
St-Sulpice
OPEN
10AM to 7PM, Tue-Sat; 2 to 7PM, Mon
NO CREDIT CARDS
$$

42. POILÂNE
Bakery

Lionel Poilâne is the best known bread baker in Paris. The Pain Poilâne sign is in the window of dozens of eateries throughout the city, and there is always a line at his own famous bakery on the Rue du Cherche-Midi. Visitors are sometimes treated to a walk through his basement kitchen where bare-chested bakers fire brick ovens filled with a dough of stone-ground flour, water, and Brittany sea salt.

It is rightly said that each batch has its own character, and though it varies, Poilâne is the standard bearer for the loaf that's crusty on the outside and mildly sour on the inside. While you're here, pick up some little shortbread cookies to stash in your purse, and consume an apple tart on the way out.

ADDRESS
8 Rue du Cherche-Midi, 6th
TELEPHONE
01.45.48.42.59
METRO
Sévres-Babylone

ADDRESS
49 Boulevard de Grenelle, 15th
TELEPHONE
01.45.79.11.49
METRO
Dupleix
OPEN
7:15AM to 8PM, Mon-Sat
NO CREDIT CARDS
$

ADDRESS
22 Rue de Sèvres, 6th
TELEPHONE
01.42.60.33.45
METRO
Sèvres-Babylone
OPEN
9:30AM to 6:30PM, Mon-Sat;
8:30AM to 8:30PM, Mon-Sat
(Food hall)
CREDIT CARDS
V, AE, MC
$$

43. LE BON MARCHE
Department store

While the fashionable right bank department stores vie for the title of "most Parisian," Le Bon Marché may win by default. This particularly unpretentious store eschews a slick image to attend to business as usual, serving its left bank clientele just as it did before the advent of "le marketing." It plays the game the old-fashioned way, with a helpful sales staff and very fair prices.

All of Paris comes here for the outstanding antiques department, a village-like arrangement of privately owned stalls, and for the Oriental rugs. The enormous food department, whose staples are peppered with specialties from around the city, is the neighborhood favorite supermarket.

ADDRESS
4 Bis Rue du Cherche-Midi, 6th
TELEPHONE
01.45.44.95.54
METRO
St-Sulpice
OPEN
10:30AM to 7PM, Mon-Sat

ADDRESS
2 Rue Tronchet, 8th
TELEPHONE
01.47.42.24.55
METRO
Madeleine
OPEN
9:30AM to 7PM, Mon-Sat
CREDIT CARDS
V, AE, DC
$$-$$$

44. ERÈS
Women's swimwear

Twice a year Erès brings in a new collection of swimsuits that actually stay up under water while you are swimming. The shop maintains its reputation as an up-to-the-minute house for beachwear design, thoughtful enough also to sell tops and bottoms separately. What more could a girl ask for? Perhaps some coordinating cover-ups: T-shirts, shawls, skirts, hooded shirts with long sleeves, and knee pants? Erès has it.

During winter they show long body suits as streetwear under the above. Most swimsuits are 700-1,100F, one piece or two, with or without cups. This is a sophisticated but simple collection, designed with many bodies in mind. If you find you need a greater choice, go to GALERIES LAFAYETTE.

45. CHANTELIVRE
Children's books

This is probably the largest children's bookstore in Paris, boasting over 10,000 volumes, and just the spot to shop for a budding francophone. Let little Mary and Johnny amuse themselves in the toy and story corner while you pursue their transformation into Marie et Jean.

For the youngest child are brightly colored hard-paged books that can be understood whatever the mother tongue. For the student are Babar (130F) and Maurice Sendak— French versions of what they have at home—which are fun and instructive since they already know the stories. The same is true for the French-language videos of Disney favorites (from 150F), but make sure they are the proper format for your VHS before you buy!

You will also find listening cassettes of French songs and stories, some English and bilingual books, and a collection of book illustration posters that includes Babar classics for 75F.

ADDRESS
13 Rue de Sèvres, 6th
TELEPHONE
01.45.48.87.90
METRO
Sévres-Babylone
OPEN
10AM to 6:30PM, Tue-Sat; 1 to 6:30PM, Mon
CREDIT CARDS
V
$$

46. CASSEGRAIN
Stationery

Since 1919, Cassegrain has been a stationer of choice for those who appreciate the dying art of fine papers. An institution among the old guard, Cassegrain continues to hand-engrave in the manner of the last century, producing calling cards and personal stationery that stand apart.

If you wish to count yourself among its overseas customers, Cassegrain will ship. Allow three weeks for engraving. Don't fail to notice the luxurious desk accessories in leather or lizard, with a lizard agenda at 2,000F, and a lizard-covered ballpoint at 350F. A smaller but equally distinctive purchase might be a box of book plates (70F) reproduced by Cassegrain from the collection at the French National Library.

ADDRESS
81 Rue des St-Pères, 6th
TELEPHONE
01.42.22.04.76
METRO
Sèvres-Babylone
OPEN
10AM to 7PM, Tue-Sat

ADDRESS
422 Rue St-Honoré, 8th
METRO
Concorde or Madeleine
TELEPHONE
01.42.60.20.08
FAX
01.42.61.40.99
OPEN
9:30AM to 6:30PM, Mon-Sat
CREDIT CARDS
V, AE, DC
$$$-$$$$

ADDRESS
71-73 Rue des St-Pères, 6th
TELEPHONE
01.45.48.88.37
METRO
Sèvres-Babylone
OPEN
10AM to 7PM, Mon-Sat
CREDIT CARDS
V, AE, DC
$$$-$$$$

47. SABBIA ROSA

Lingerie

This is where French starlets often come for their most glamorous underthings, so when you are planning an evening of stardom you'll want to stop here. The seamstresses downstairs stitch luxurious little nothings from silk satins, handworked Calais lace, and fine-gauge cottons.

With patterned bras (700F) that can hold their own under an evening shawl, to Brazilian-style undies (600F), to sultry satin pajamas, you'll have no problem changing even the most modest image at Mme Rosa's. If you don't find what you had in mind, the workshop will be happy to whip it up for you.

ADDRESS
63 Rue des St-Pères, 6th
TELEPHONE
01.45.49.30.37
METRO
Sèvres-Babylone
CREDIT CARDS
V, AE, MC
$$-$$$

48. SHADÉ

Costume jewelry and accessories

The fresh vision of Marilyn Sfadj brings what's new and stylish from both the designer studios and the craftsman's atelier to her elegant little boutique, a gentlewoman's shop from the marble floor to the romantic chandelier.

Besides pieces from the likes of Lacroix, Lagerfeld, Kenzo, and Dior are handcrafted items she has sought around France, many unique to her. A hair barrette decorated with hand-dyed and hand-sewn fabric buds took the artist three hours to make and sells for 390F, with matching earrings for 240F. There are bags, sunglasses, and lots of hair and jewelry pieces to catch your fancy.

49. DEBAUVE & GALLAIS
Chocolates and teas

Founded as a pharmacy in 1800, Debauve & Gallais
began dispensing chocolates as a medicine to such
eminents as King Charles X, and later to Napoleon. It's
certainly worth a stop, even if you're not a chocoholic.

While the chocolates are a bit sweet for my taste
(though children adore them), the decor remains that
of an 18th-century apothecary, with candies enticingly
displayed in semicircular wooden pharmaceutical cases,
potted ferns, marble columns, and the original scales
and tea boxes.

ADDRESS
30 Rue des St-Prés, 7th
TELEPHONE
01.45.48.54.67
METRO
St-Germain-des-Près
OPEN
10AM to 1PM & 2 to 7PM, Tue-
Fri; 10AM to 1PM & 2 to 6PM,
Sat
Closed last week of July and
throughout August
NO CREDIT CARDS
$$

50. CHARLES KAMMER
Women's shoes

These very style-oriented shoes are grabbed up by
shoeaholics as well as by everyone else who likes to
dress up her feet. The prices here make it easy to walk
out with a closetful of moods from straight-laced to
embroidered baroque, all of a quality that may even
outlast the style.

ADDRESS
14 Rue de Grenelle, 7th
TELEPHONE
01.42.22.91.19
METRO
St-Sulpice
OPEN
10AM to 7PM, Mon-Sat
CREDIT CARDS
V, AE
$$-$$$

51. THE GENERAL STORE
American food items

Can't get through another day abroad without your
Doritos? Ready to trade in your morning croissant for
a box of Aunt Jemima's Pancake Mix? After gorging
yourself in the finest European chocolate shops do you
still crave a Hershey Bar? Rest assured you'll find the
goodies here to satisfy your American taste, but be
prepared to pay through the nose for them.

The General Store is the junk food junkie's French
fix, and a mainstay for Americans living in Paris who
need their pumpkin pie filling for Thanksgiving and
chocolate chip cookies after school. Let the French
proprietor here advise you on his California wines.

ADDRESS
82 Rue de Grenelle, 7th
TELEPHONE
01.45.48.63.16
METRO
Rue du Bac
OPEN
10AM to 7PM, Mon-Sat
CREDIT CARDS
V, AE, DC
$$$$ (compared to back home)

ADDRESS
84 Bis Rue de Grenelle, 7th
TELEPHONE
01.45.44.61.57
METRO
Rue du Bac

ADDRESS
5 Rue des Capucines, 1st
TELEPHONE
01.42.96.35.13
FAX
01.41.19.06.31
METRO
Opéra
OPEN
10AM to 7PM, Mon-Sat
CREDIT CARDS
V, AE, MC, DC
$$$

52. MAITRE PARFUMEUR ET GANTIER
Fragrances and gloves

When the infallible "nose" Jean Laporte profitably sold off his last successful enterprise (L'Artisan Parfumeur), he claimed it took no more than a walk in his garden in Bourgogne for him to invent an entirely new line of fragrances for women, men, and the home, sold exclusively in these beautifully restored 18th-century shops. In the manner of the period, they are offered alongside a collection of perfumed gloves.

If you want to avoid the commercial scents one smells everywhere in Paris, and that even your Parisian taxi driver will recognize, come here for an hour well spent exploring original and subtle compositions with a salesperson who speaks English and guides your search for a fragrance that projects the real you. Eau-de-toilette is sold here, not perfume, and yes, it does last until your evening bath. The 30-plus scents are of the highest quality and sell for around 300F a bottle. If, in true Parisienne style, you seek a lifelong fragrance that to your friends and family will become synonymous with you, the boutiques will continue to fill your orders by mail within 10 days. Be sure to pick up their mail-order brochures for both personal and household fragrances. Also worth reordering are beautifully boxed soaps (35F), large lingerie sachets in moire pockets (120F), bath oils (160F), candles in glass (135F), and the extraordinary *montgolfiers*—hand-chiseled terra cotta balls filled with a scented resin that evaporates over a period of years in your home (120 to 480F). Once you've lived with Laporte scents, you'll keep writing back for more.

53. DINERS EN VILLE
Table arts

This is the best spot in Paris to inspire your table, and you'll come away full of fresh ideas along with the treasures in your shopping bag. When the Comtesse de Mandat Grancey first displayed a table mixing old with new in place settings, a taboo was broken. Parisian hostesses embraced the license to dress their dining table with more room for whimsy and a smaller pocketbook. It is now considered not only acceptable, but smart to set your table with great-grandmother's silver and antique-reproduction china, and here you'll find everything you need to achieve that look.

The Countess has gathered charming examples of old- and new-fashioned glassware, flatware, dishes, linens, and centerpieces, much of it elegantly arranged on tables set throughout the store. Each of many rooms has shelves packed with pieces in moods from country to lavish, Empire to Deco. Be sure to take the rear staircase to the second floor, devoted to trompe l'oeil dishes and tea services. Even if you already have enough in flatware and china settings, you will be tempted to grab up collectibles like the antique silver fruit spoons (120F) and stylish paisley tablecloths (from 700F). You'll find accessory pieces galore here, and the whole so distinctive that you may miss dinner trying to narrow down your choices.

ADDRESS
27 Rue de Varenne & 89 Rue du Bac (2 entrances), 7th
TELEPHONE
01.42.22.78.33
METRO
Rue du Bac
OPEN
10AM to 7PM, Tue-Sat
CREDIT CARDS
V
$$$

ADDRESS
63 Rue du Bac, 7th
TELEPHONE
01.42.22.03.16
FAX
01.42.84.12.47
METRO
Rue du Bac
OPEN
9:30AM to 6:30PM, Mon-Sat
CREDIT CARDS
V, AE
$$$

54. ETAMINE
Home decorating

Ever since this shop opened it has been jammed with Parisians looking to escape the cultural baggage of their French decorating traditions and embrace the new international style. I might point out that most tourists to France still appreciate the old in French style, so to fully appreciate the Etamine phenomenon, you must think like a young Parisian who is encumbered with inherited furnishings from previous centuries and perhaps even with an ornate family apartment.

The stylists here travel the world for inspiration, designing a new collection of fabrics and wallpapers, small furniture pieces, dishes, vases, lamps, bedroom and table linens every three months, then move on to another geographic passion. Likewise, entering the shop can be a visit to a country cottage, or a safari to Africa. Whatever the collection of the moment, the individual arrangements are put together in a manner purely Etamine, displaying classically French good taste.

Etamine

ADDRESS
101 Rue du Bac, 7th
METRO
Rue du Bac
TELEPHONE
01.42.22.89.48
OPEN
10AM to 7PM, Tue-Sat; 1 to 7PM, Mon
CREDIT CARDS
V
$$$

55. DENISE BOURILLON
Women's clothing

Envision yourself wrapped in a long knit skirt and sweater under a heavy reversible cape, strolling the foggy banks of the Seine, and outfit yourself at Bourillon. The handmade knits from the workshop downstairs are all designed by M. Denise, as he is called, and are found exclusively here where he has woven his ideas into sophisticated garments for 18 years.

Everything is knitted from silk, wool, or cotton yarns in rich tones tending toward the earthy and deep jewels, sometimes touched with gold. So stroll the Seine costumed as above or pull a light-weight knit T-shirt over your jeans. You'll feel eternally feminine in these timeless designs.

56. BONPOINT

Children's clothing, shoes, and furniture
Maternity (Rue de l'Université only)

Founded by sisters not so long ago, Bonpoint has become an instant classic. The sweetly dressed darlings in carriages adorned with Alsacian lace and pique from the layette collection grow up to shop for their flannels and tweeds, or pleated skirts and velvet vests (760 to 860F) at Bonpoint Junior for ages 12 to 18. They spend the years between shuttling in and out of the boutique at N.67 with Nanny, admiring the young ladies and gentlemen in the displays who are smartly attired in velvet gloves and lace collars. The rough-and-ready look is here, too, in the refined forms of a soft leather bomber jacket with sweater and lined cords or western wear. The Rue de l'Université location is doubtless the best stop in Paris for a complete child's wardrobe that is elegant, sophisticated, and exceedingly well made, with furnishings down the street, and the small discount store selling last year's collection just a few blocks away. At Bonpoint even a window stop is worthwhile.

Bonpoint

ADDRESS
67 Rue de l'Université, 7th
TELEPHONE
01.45.55.63.70
METRO
Solférino

ADDRESS
86 Rue de l'Université, 7th
(Bonpoint Junior)
TELEPHONE
01.45.51.17.68
METRO
Solférino

ADDRESS
7 Rue de Solférino, 7th
(Furniture)
TELEPHONE
01.45.55.42.79
METRO
Solférino

ADDRESS
15 Rue Royale, 8th
TELEPHONE
01.47.42.52.63
METRO
Madeleine

ADDRESS
64 Avenue Raymond Poincarré,
16th
TELEPHONE
01.47.27.60.81
METRO
Victor-Hugo
OPEN
10AM to 7PM, Mon-Sat
CREDIT CARDS
V, AE
$$$-$$$$

ADDRESS
82 Rue de Grenelle, 7th
(Outlet store)
TELEPHONE
01.47.48.05.45
METRO
Bac
OPEN
10AM to12:30PM & 1 to 6PM,
Mon-Sat
NO CREDIT CARDS
$-$$

Bonpoint

ADDRESS
4 Rue du Pré-aux-Clercs, 7th
TELEPHONE
01.42.61.71.60
METRO
St-Germain-des-Prés
OPEN
10AM to 7PM, Mon-Sat
CREDIT CARDS
V
$$-$$$

57. CORINNE SARRUT
Women's clothing

Sarrut style epitomizes what the French call "the classics revisited." Known for her berets in fashionable colors (150F), cigarette pants in her fabrics of the season (600F in denim), and structured wool pullovers that work well under coordinating jackets (1,500F), the young designer always has a good selection of separates in basic colors. Don't overlook the silk dresses, but be advised that this is a boutique for the figure that requires no alterations.

ADDRESS
6 Rue du Pré-aux-Clercs, 7th
TELEPHONE
01.40.20.44.12
METRO
St-Germaine-des-Prés
OPEN
10:30AM to 1:30PM & 2:30 to 7PM, Mon-Fri; 10:30AM to 7:30PM, Sat
CREDIT CARDS
V, AE, MC, DC
$$-$$$

58. LES PRAIRIES DE PARIS
Women's clothing

Here is a shop for the sophisticate who prefers the simple cut of the ingenue in her streetwear. There is very little color to distract from the line of these discrete dresses and separates in lambskin, velours or tweeds. The stylist here spent 29 years at Barney's, and has developed a collection of easy-to-sport basics that are quite charming.

59. LAURENCE TAVERNIER
Men's and women's loungewear

While you're busy investigating wardrobe possibilities on the rest of the street, send monsieur ahead to scout out something immensely relaxed for the two of you to don in your chamber. The Tavernier collection is sober and civilized, yet modern in its choice of color and simple detail. He may choose for himself a well-styled nightshirt or pajamas of shirting cotton in any of 27 colors (810F), with cashmere slippers.

And for you, choose perhaps a ruffled-cuff nightshirt with a shawl for cool nights in front of the fire. If he's not with you this is a good stop for an intimate gift: the men's collection also includes underwear and swim trunks.

ADDRESS
7 Rue du Prés-aux-Clercs, 7th
TELEPHONE
01.49.27.03.95
METRO
St-Germain-des-Prés
OPEN
10AM to 7PM, Mon-Sat
CREDIT CARDS
V
$$$

Laurence Tavernier

60. NATHALIE GARÇON
Women's clothing

Nathalie Garçon has been a favorite of *Elle* magazine since her first collection appeared a decade ago in Paris department stores. Now that her standout look has its own boutique, women who love her brilliant colors and natural fabrics can choose their suits, dresses and everyday dressing in a calmer setting. This is a popular address with *Parisiennes* who prefer a silhouette that tends toward a generous cut.

ADDRESS 11
Rue du Pré-aux-Clercs, 7th
TELEPHONE
01.45.48.41.72
METRO
St-Germaine-des-Prés
OPEN
11:30AM to 7PM, Mon-Sat
CREDIT CARDS
V, AE, MC
$$$

ADDRESS
8 Rue du Pré-aux-Clercs, 7th (2 entrances)
TELEPHONE
01.42.61.18.28
METRO
St-Germain-des-Prés
OPEN
10AM to 7PM, Mon-Sat
CREDIT CARDS
V, AE, MC
$$-$$$

61. IRIÉ
Women's clothing

There is a reason why well-dressed women from 15 to 50 stop in here weekly, and why it appears to be among the most popular clothing boutiques in Paris. It's cheap chic, with the emphasis on chic, and it's abundant in these designs by Japanese-born, Kenzo-trained, Parisian-minded Irié. Refreshingly original, charming, and comfortable, his collection is born of contrasts: a refined tea suit cut in a bottom-hugging stretch fabric, quiet wool blazers in loud colors, and chameleon-like tight little skirts that take on the demeanor of whatever they accompany. Perhaps the sharpest contrast of all is the solemn Italian interior, filled with marble, music, and black lacquer piano under a low white ceiling.

ADDRESS
10 Rue du Pré-aux-Clercs, 7th
TELEPHONE
01.42.22.89.63
METRO
St-Germain-des-Prés
OPEN
2 to 7PM, Mon; 10AM to 7PM, Tue-Sat
CREDIT CARDS
V
$$-$$$

62. ISADORA
Costume jewelry

These bright and chunky baubles are full of fun and character. Isadora works exclusively on Bakelite, a hard plastic-like material developed in the 1930s. But the product is nothing retro. What she began 15 years ago as witty, figurative jewelry now includes many modern geometrics in stark black and white or vivid colors.

In her studio, Isadora cuts her material from sheets, dying and rubbing it to perfection, while her mother handles sales to a loyal clientele that includes the Los Angeles County Museum gift shop. Prices and selection are best at the source with earrings beginning at 250F, necklaces at 750 to 1,300F, and rings and bracelets in between. She also has a nice collection of costume jewelry from 1900 through the 1950s.

☕ AUX DEUX MAGOTS
Café

ADDRESS
170 Boulevard St- Germain, 6th
TELEPHONE
01.45.48.55.25
METRO
St-Germain-des-Prés
OPEN
8AM to 2PM daily
$$$

Aux Deux Magots has possibly the most inviting sidewalk cafe in the city. Come here while you're waiting for your hotel room to be readied. No matter how jet-lagged you may feel, you'll know you're in Paris when you arrive here.

Inside, mirrored walls, red banquettes, snappily turned-out waiters, and the ghosts of Sartre and Hemingway, who both had tables here, epitomize cafe life. Settle in over a frothy *café au lait* and people watch to catch up on fashion trends before embarking on your Left Bank shopping tour. Just next door at 172 Boulevard St-Germain is the equally popular CAFE DE FLORE.

63. MADELEINE GELY
Umbrellas and canes

ADDRESS
218 Boulevard St-Germain, 7th
TELEPHONE
01.42.22.63.35
METRO
St-Germain-des-Près
OPEN
9:30AM to 7PM, Tue-Sat; closed August
CREDIT CARDS
V
$$-$$$

Umbrellas and canes have been walking out of this tiny shop since 1834, and it's undoubtedly the most famous of its kind in Paris. Mme Gély's umbrellas are made exclusively for her, most in the establishment's original styles. Though the umbrella may be new, it could have been appropriate for a gentleman 150 years ago, or for a modern gentlewoman.

For the littlest mademoiselle, don't overlook the pink folding parasol with the green frog handle (437F). There are antique and collector pieces as well as reproductions—umbrellas and canes with handles in carved wood, bamboo, or molded synthetic. You may choose one with fold-out spectacles or a hidden whiskey flask, or an animal head from her zoological garden. These aren't necessarily the cumbersome loads of yesteryear. Many will fold into a purse or satchel and Madame offers a handsome array of her own umbrella fabrics which she is happy to match to a handle of your choosing.

ADDRESS
175 Boulevard St-Germain, 6th
(Women's clothing and accessories)
TELEPHONE
01.49.54.60.60
METRO
St-Germain-des-Prés

ADDRESS
70 Faubourg St-Honoré, 8th
(Women's)
TELEPHONE
01.42.65.20.81
METRO
Concorde

ADDRESS
194 Boulevard St-Germain, 6th
(Men)
TELEPHONE
01.45.44.83.19
METRO
St-Germain-des-Prés

ADDRESS
4 Rue de Grenelle, 7th
(Children)
TELEPHONE
01.49.54.61.10
METRO
St-Sulpice

ADDRESS
6 Rue de Grenelle, 7th
(Inscriptions)
TELEPHONE
01.49.54.61.00
METRO
St-Sulpice
OPEN
10AM to 7PM, Mon-Sat
CREDIT CARDS
V, AE, DC
$$$

SR (OUTLET)
ADDRESS
64 Rue d'Alésia, 14th
TELEPHONE
01.43.95.06.13
METRO
Alésia
OPEN
2 to 7PM, Mon; 10AM to 7PM,
Tue-Sat
$$

64. SONIA RYKIEL
Women's, men',s and children's clothing & home items

The architect of the skinny knit has built a modern *château* worthy of her elegant collections. Her St-Germain headquarters showcasing women's clothing and accessories and porcelain for the table are large, light, and easy to shop in. Here you will find her trademark knits in cotton and wool, understated in color and shape, but dramatic in effect and always comfortable. The look is true Parisian chic, and it's made to travel. Pack her culottes, tight sweater, and jersey jacket in your carry on, throw on some of her gold jewelry, and you could land anywhere in style. Her collection has expanded to velours and other simple fabrics.

The original small shop at 4 Rue de Grenelle is home to Sonia's delightful fashions for the modern child. Next door at N.6 is the moderately priced Inscriptions line designed by her daughter Natalie for the jeans and T-shirt set.

SONIA RYKIEL HOMME, the comfy men's store on Rue Perronet, offers a complete wardrobe for the modern monsieur.

65. DANIEL HECHTER
Men's and women's clothing

The sporty, classic look of the French preppy is easy to buy at these stores. With such fastidious tailoring, how do the prices stay so reasonable? That's the Hechter touch. If he cuts corners anywhere, it's occasionally with less than natural fabrics, but even these models come out looking well bred.

The newest boutique, on Rue François I, has a comfy ambiance lacking in the others. For men I recommend the modern warmth of the Rue Tronchet boutique, complete with bar, and poems scrawled across dressing room walls. The outlet store offers what's left of last season's collection at 30 percent off.

ADDRESS
146 Boulevard St-Germain, 6th
METRO
Odéon
TELEPHONE
01.43.26.96.36

ADDRESS
2 Place de Passy, 16th
TELEPHONE
01.42.88.01.11
METRO
La Muette or Passy

ADDRESS
31 Rue Tronchet, 8th (Men's line only)
TELEPHONE
01.42.65.56.76
METRO
Havre-Caumartin
OPEN
10AM to 7PM, Mon-Sat
CREDIT CARDS
V, AE, DC
$$-$$$

ADDRESS
66 Rue François I, 8th
TELEPHONE
01.40.70.94.38
METRO
Georges V or Alma-Marceau
OPEN
10:30AM to 7:30PM, Mon-Sat
CREDIT CARDS
V, AE, DC
$$-$$$

STOCK 2 (OUTLET)
ADDRESS
92 Rue d'Alésia, 14th
TELEPHONE
01.45.41.65.57
METRO
Alésia
OPEN
10AM to 7PM, Mon-Sat
NO CREDIT CARDS
$$

ADDRESS
34 Boulevard St-Germain, 5th
TELEPHONE
01.43.26.45.27
METRO
Maubert-Mutualité
OPEN
10AM to 7PM, Tue-Sat
CREDIT CARDS
V
$$

66. DIPTYQUE
Scented candles, soaps, and toilette waters

Candles in 32 natural scents, good prices, and lovely packaging make this boutique a worthwhile stop for gift givers or for those who want the familiar fragrances of France in their own homes.

Begin with *foin coupé* (fresh-cut hay) or *chevrefeuille* (honeysuckle) before you take on heavier scents such as lavenders and musks. The white-glassed candles burn for 60 hours, slower in cold temperatures, faster where it's warm. Buy more than one, because once you become used to these scents at home, you won't be able to live without them.

ADDRESS
98 Rue Monge, 5th (Entrance on Rue Daubenton)
TELEPHONE
01.43.31.16.42
METRO
Censier-Daubenton
OPEN
10:30AM to 7PM, Tue-Sat
$$

67. LA LIBRARIE DES GOURMETS
Cookbooks

This pleasant and well-lit shop makes a convenient stop for cooks coming from LA TUILE A LOUP across the way. Specializing in French books about French cooking, eating, and drinking, the selection of beautiful photographic books showing French foods as they are meant to be served is inspirational.

For the galloping gourmet are food and wine maps of France with pictures and descriptions of regional specialties. Of course there is a shelf of English books on restaurants in Paris.

If you want to leave France a little wiser in the ways of the bottle, take a look at Le Nez du Vin (the nose for wine), nicely boxed scent kits teaching you to recognize the grape odors found in wines. A kit for champagne, teaching 12 regional components, is 435F, while a basic wine kit of 6 scents is 150F.

68. LA TUILE A LOUP
Pottery and handcrafted tableware from around France

Make only a slight detour from central Paris to discover these regional table arts of France, guaranteed to degentrify your dining. The Joblin-Depalle family travels throughout the French countryside to bring works from the finest traditional ceramic craftsmen, glassblowers, and basket-weavers to this rustic urban outpost, a well-known source for nearly extinct crafts. In a recent year, the shop lost 35 suppliers who could no longer find enough market for their work.

Large wooden tables are stacked high with pottery plates and bowls of various shapes and shades, which to the learned eye represent the clays and glazes of rural France. Choose from the exceptional baskets and fill them with handblown glasses from a factory established in 1475 (68F), earthy egg cups (40F), and an olivewood cheese tray. Or pick a large urn from Provence and a dozen settings of glazed earthenware dinner plates from the Savoie, and let the establishment do the shipping. You may want to call ahead to make sure the owners, who speak English, will be in. If you read French, take a look at the selection of books on French regional history and customs. The trip here is well worth it.

ADDRESS
35 Rue Daubenton, 5th
TELEPHONE
01.47.07.28.90
METRO
Censier-Daubenton
OPEN
10:30AM to 1PM & 3 to 7:30PM, Tue-Sat; 10:30AM to 1PM, Sun
CREDIT CARDS
V, AE
$$

☕ BRASSERIE BALZAR
Bistro

ADDRESS
49 Rue des Ecoles, 5th
TELEPHONE
01.43.54.13.67
METRO
Maubert-Mutualité
OPEN
Noon to 12:30AM daily; closed August
CREDIT CARDS
V
$$

When a jaded Left Bank Parisian longs for the tummy-soothing experience of days past, he'll head for the Balzar, a thoroughly authentic example of the classic Parisian bistro that has defied modern trends without a tarnish to its well-shined mirrors and mahogany.

Order a roast chicken with sautéed spinach and fries and you'll understand the meaning of comfort food. Or consider the plates on their way to your neighbors' tables. For an amiable mix of food and company, you can't go wrong here. Reserve for dinner.

ADDRESS
37 Rue de la Bucherie, 5th
TELEPHONE
01.43.26.96.50
METRO
Maubert-Mutualité
OPEN
Noon to midnight, Mon-Sun
NO CREDIT CARDS
$-$$

69. SHAKESPEARE AND COMPANY
Books

The inscription stamped on the inside cover of every book purchased here reads, "Shakespeare and Company Kilometer Zero Paris." And this is indeed the heart of the city for students, writers, readers, and browsers who frequently stop in to read and rub shoulders with their own kind.

Over 40 years ago George Whitman opened his doors to lovers of the English written word, selling mostly secondhand volumes from England and America. In name and in spirit the shop reflects an earlier bookstore run by American Sylvia Beach that became a gathering place for expatriate writers such as Hemingway and Fitzgerald. It was Sylvia Beach who dared to publish James Joyce's *Ulysses*.

Whitman's small shop across from Notre Dame has an appropriately homey air of comfortable confusion and is a must stop for anyone with a fascination for our expatriate writers, particularly if you need a good read for the trip home. And who knows? If you pen a good line he just may invite you to stay on for a few days in his writer's room, to carry on a grand tradition.

Along the Way

Some of my most sentimental purchases have been from the BOUQUINISTES (booksellers) along the quais on both banks of the Seine. From mid-morning until dusk these collectors of old books, maps, prints, and post cards open their stalls to lookers and buyers alike, who are free to poke through their treasures. Most have their specialties.

If you're in the market for a first-edition Colette, surrealist post cards or a hand-colored poster of Marie Antoinette, you have a good chance of finding them here. Open Tue-Sat, or at the whim of the free-spirited vendor.

THE ISLANDS

The historical and geographical heart of Paris lies between the left and right banks of the Seine on two small islands, the ILE DE LA CITÉ and the ILE ST-LOUIS, joined by the bridge PONT ST-LOUIS. It was on the wild Ile de la Cité that a tribe of fishermen calling themselves Parisii came to settle in the 3rd century BC.

Today these are two islands of relative serenity in the Seine captured in time between the modern bustle of the left and right banks. The islands are a good spot to catch your breath after a whirlwind shopping tour, or to spend a Sunday when most of the rest of the city is closed down.

On a Sunday, head to the Ile de la Cité to attend the 10:30AM mass at NOTRE DAME, or plan on the 5:45PM organ concert. Perhaps you'll catch a candle-lit concert at SAINT CHAPELLE (4 Boulevard du Palais), a gothic chapel with dazzling acoustics, stained glass, and starlit ceiling.

The famous flower market (open daybreak to 4PM, Mon-Sat) at PLACE LOUIS LEP-INE becomes the famous bird market on Sundays (9AM to 7PM). Stop in at FANNY TEA, N.20 Place Dauphine (open 1 to 7:30PM, Tue-Fri and 3:30 to 8PM, Sat-Sun) for tea, tart and poetic ambiance. On this island, shopping is limited to the souvenir stands.

Cross over to the Ile St-Louis, which wakes up early Sunday afternoons to enjoy its reputation as one of the only open shopping areas in Paris. If you're really hungry, stop at the BRASSERIE DE L'ILE ST-LOUIS, N. 55 Quai de Bourbon (open noon to 1AM, Fri-Tue and Thurs dinner) for Alsatian choucroñte (sausage-garnished sauerkraut) and beer, shoulder-to-shoulder with the regulars, and be prepared to make new friends.

It is said that there are local residents who never leave the island. And why not? It is among the choicest addresses in the city, and its outstanding 17th-century hôtels partic-uliers (private residences) are inhabited by the Baron de Rothschild and the pretender to the throne of France, whose once-royal family still doesn't celebrate Bastille Day.

Pick up an ice cream or sorbet from BERTHILLON, the best in Paris and sold at nearly every café and tea salon on the island as well as the original store, N. 31 Rue St-Louis-en-Ile, and you're on your way down the main street. Rue St-Louis-en-Ile is only a few short blocks, and given over to souvenir shops and galleries as well as necessities for local residents, so prepare to browse.

PYLONES, N.57 Rue St-Louis-en-Ile, carries its own brand of humorous suspenders and neckties, made of latex and just the right thing to lighten up that tuxedo. You'll con-gratulate yourself on your good taste when you see more of the same in the gift shop at the Pompidou Center. YAMINA, N.56 Rue St-Louis-en-Ile, specializes in hand-painted scarves and women's clothing.

Up the street is ALLO-ALLO, where you can find useful upscale souvenirs like bread knives in baguette-shaped holders, and metal model kits of the Tour Eiffel. At LE GRAIN DE SABLE, N.79 Rue St-Louis-en-Ile, choose from among thousands of beads, and pick cord and clasp, to make your own chic Parisian fantasy jewelry or choose from what the salespeople string together in their spare time.

Rive Droite

The Right Bank is where you'll find the *crème de la crème*. If you are most comfortable in a setting of grand hotels, luxurious boutiques, *couture* labels, and first-rate service, begin your shopping tour here. From the Ritz to Dior, from Christofle to Hermès, you'll recognize names that have set standards of taste for generations.

Even if you consider yourself more of a Left Bank type, don't miss this opportunity to explore the prestigious addresses of the Right Bank. For an education in classically French fashion, art, and home furnishings, make your way down the Avenue Montaigne and the Faubourg Saint-Honoré, the Rue Royale, and the Place Vendôme. The dazzling window displays along these boulevards will turn your head and capture your imagination, and you're bound to come away with something ineffably French.

For more intimate shopping and less intimidating price tags, visit the elegant Palais Royale and neighboring arcades. Join the French to discover the next trend in fashion at the Place des Victoires, and shop where they do in the renovated region of Les Halles, the former city market where cutting utensils still take their place next to the latest cuts in clothing.

Where to Stay

The Right Bank is full of wonderful grand hotels, with the incomparable Hotel Ritz an inspiration to all that follow. But if money is a consideration, you'll find better values elsewhere. For convenience sake, here are two more moderately priced luxury hotels in the heart of the golden triangle.

ADDRESS
239 Rue St-Honoré, 1st
TELEPHONE
01.42.44.50.00
FAX
01.42.44.50.01
METRO
Tuilleries
Double rooms from 1,590F
CREDIT CARDS
V, AE, MC, DC

HOTEL COSTES

The hotel of the moment, Hotel Costes shuns the minimalism of the past decade to flaunt its georgeous interiors that teeter the fine line between Napoleonic luxe and Italian bordello. Yes, models and stars stay here, and are often visible as all dining areas and bars look onto the interior courtyard where meals are served in fine weather. American guests will further appreciate here that rarity in Paris, a fitness center and pool.

ADDRESS
37 Rue François I, 8th
TELEPHONE
01.47.23.54.42
FAX
01.47.23.08.84
METRO
Alma-Marçeau
Double Rooms from 1250F;
Breakfast 70F
CREDIT CARDS
V, AE

HOTEL CLARIDGE-BELLMAN

I always enjoy this small deluxe hotel, perfectly located for shopping the Avenue Montaigne. You'll find it quiet and well appointed with rich furnishings inherited from the former Claridge Hotel. The dining room is lovely, though breakfast is more reasonable anywhere else in the neighborhood.

HÔTEL MONTAIGNE

The Hôtel Montaigne offers every modern amenity in the discretely luxurious surroundings you would expect to find in this location. A very personal reception welcomes every guest by name. The larger, quieter rooms are over the courtyard. Take your breakfast or grab a bite anytime at the Bar des Théatres next door.

ADDRESS
6 Avenue Montaigne, 8th
TELEPHONE
01.47.20.30.50
FAX
01.47.20.94.12
METRO
Alma-Marçeau
Doubles from 1600F; breakfast 65F
CREDIT CARDS
V, AE

REGINA

An old-world hotel, the Regina is loved for her enormous rooms filled with period pieces, some overlooking the Louvre and Tuileries Gardens. In the stately lobby of this quiet hotel, beautiful old clocks keep time for the major European capitals.

ADDRESS
2 Place des Pyramides, 1st
TELEPHONE
01.42.60.31.10
FAX
01.40.15.95.16
METRO
Tuileries
Double rooms from 1,600F
CREDIT CARDS
V, AE, MC

Culture Along the Way

TUILERIES GARDINS

These former gardens of King Louis XIV run from his palace (now the Louvre Museum) to the Place de La Concorde. A stroll through its manicured hedges and bronze statues offers respite from the nearby crowds and a vantage point for a clear view through the Arc de Triomphe to the new Arche de La Défense. Its JEU DE PAUME MUSEUM, once Paris's impressionist museum, now exhibits contemporary art. Gates open at 9AM and close at dusk.

MÉTRO:
Concorde or Tuileries

ADDRESS
107 Rue de Rivoli, 1st
METRO
Palais-Royal or Tuileries or
Louvre

MUSÉE DES ARTS DECORATIFS

You'll learn more about historically correct and avant-garde interiors here than by thumbing the pages of a lifetime's worth of decorating magazines. The museum for the decorative arts shows French interiors from medieval times to present-day. Open 11AM-6PM, Sat; 10AM to 6PM, Sun; Wed until 9PM. Closed Mon.

ADDRESS
107 Rue de Rivoli, 1st
METRO
Palais-Royal or Tuileries or
Louvre

MUSÉE DES ARTS DE LA MODE ET DU TEXTILE

Newly reopened in the Rohan wing of the Louvre, three floors of fashions and costumes worn by French men and women of all classes and regions from medieval times to modern-day are shown in period settings, including proud collections of *haute couture*. Open 11AM to 6PM, Tue-Fri; 10AM to 6PM, Sat-Sun; closed Mon.

ADDRESS
Enter through glass Pyramid
off Cour Napoléon, 1st
METRO
Palais-Royal or Tuileries or
Louvre

MUSÉE NATIONAL DU LOUVRE

Europe's largest palace holds collections from ancient times to mid-19th-century. Need one say more? Open 9AM to 6 PM, Mon, Thurs-Sun; Wed until 9:45PM; closed Tue.

ADDRESS
120 Rue Saint-Martin, 4th
MÉTRO
Hôtel-de-Ville

MUSEE NATIONAL D'ART MODERNE (POMPIDOU CENTER)

The most visited attraction in France not only contains the national collection of 20th-century art in a controversial modern structure, but has a priceless view over the rooftops of Paris from the top floor. Open noon-10PM; Sat, Sun, and holidays 10AM to 10PM; closed Tue. The museum has been closed for structural repairs. Make sure it has reopened before your visit.

Right Bank Shops

The neighborhood flanked by the Avenue Montaigne, the Rue François I, and the Avenue Georges V is known as the GOLDEN TRIANGLE, and as you stroll down the Avenue Montaigne in particular, you'll know why. The enormous chic is matched only by the price tags. Nobody treats fine merchandise quite as well as the French do, so whether you're buyer or browser, don't hesitate to step through those intimidating facades and explore a little.

Avenue Montaigne

If you buy here, you'll carry away with you a true Parisian luxury, wrapped so beautifully you may never want to open it. Rarely too crowded, particularly during the week, this is my favorite area for luxury goods, and there are always some very good buys.

☕ BAR DES THEATRES

ADDRESS
6 Ave. Montaigne, 8th
TELEPHONE
01.47.23.34.63
METRO
Alma-Marçeau
OPEN
6:00AM to 2AM daily

Bar Des Théâtres

This popular restautrant-bar is open and hopping 20 hours a day, frequented by waves of actors, musicians, and technicians from the Théâtre des Champs Elysées across the street, giving way to locals and well-heeled shoppers during normal business hours. The sophisticated mix is part of its charm, and so are the reliable meals and quick service. On theatre nights you must reserve a table or come at 8PM when the place clears out for showtime. For lunch, arrive early or wait in line and watch the orders go by, or grab a quick sandwich at the bar. I highly recommend the *tarte tatin* (an upside-down apple pie) with *crème fraîche*.

ADDRESS
14 Avenue Montaigne, 8th
TELEPHONE
01.47.23.08.94
FAX
01.47.23.05.54
METRO
Alma-Marçeau
OPEN
10AM to 7PM, Mon-Sat
CREDIT CARDS
V, AE, MC
$$$

1. INES DE LA FRESSANGE
Women's clothing, shoes, costume jewelry, linens, luggage

To this promenade of old-world taste and new world money comes the fresh view of younger-minded aristocrat Inès de la Fressange. Formerly top model for Chanel, her personal style was inspiration to its superstar designer Karl Lagerfeld. When the French government honored her by requesting to make her the official face of France, or "Marianne," as the French call this tradition, she accepted and was immediately dropped by Chanel. It didn't take long for her to launch herself into the store project, carrying out her own designs in her relaxed uniform of narrow black trousers, white shirt, blazer, and ballerina flats; a famous face whose dark eyes and red lips are set off under cropped black hair.

The lighthearted interior by family friend and noted furniture designer Alexis de la Falaise is certainly an antidote to this serious street, with its plank walls painted in pinks, greens, yellows, and blues that reflect Inès' preference for an upbeat, pared-down look that has been adopted by an entire generation of well-bred French women who want a more casual look than their mothers.

The store sells her own designs, classic, quality clothes at reasonable prices; distinctive costume jewelry, some in the form of her signature oak leaf; versions of her ballerina flat in silk, leather, and velour, under a hanging crystal ship in the shoe and handbag salon; hemstitched linen and damask bedding; hand-thrown glassware; even dog collars.

If you want an understated look that speaks with a husky French accent, get in line and let Inès's sales staff help you put it together.

2. DROUOT MONTAIGNE
Auction house of fine art and antiques

Drouot Montaigne is the newest, most expensive, and to my knowing French friends, "the best" branch of the renowned Paris auction house Drouot. In keeping with the address, you'll find the most prestigious sales at this location. Not that the original Hotel Drouot isn't brimming with treasures, and with professional dealers.

To browse or to buy, first pick up a copy of the weekly auction guide "La Gazette de L'Hotel Drouot" at any newsstand, and an auction catalog that schedules and defines every lot, at the front desk. Arrive early enough to visit each room before bidding so you can get your bearings and determine how active you plan to be. Registration isn't necessary. The bidding is fast and in French, so you should be equipped with a calculator and possibly a translator (available through the front desk).

Keep in mind the 10 to 18 percent commission you'll be paying the house above the bid price, and the cost of shipping. The house will suggest the transporter Jet Art Services (ph: 01.45.23.38.39) to be called before storage fees on your purchases accrue (after 24 hours).

It is best to pay cash for your merchandise, avoiding possible shipping delays waiting for a check to clear; the in-house bank can help you with currency exchange.

If you're feeling mystified, hold on to that vision of the chandelier from the Paris Opera above your dining table and go for it. The auction system here is highly professional and so are your bidding competitors, so keep your wits about you and remember, not only are these heirlooms the real thing, they're also at wholesale prices.

ADDRESS
15 Avenue Montaigne, 8th
TELEPHONE
01.48.00.20.80
METRO
Alma-Marçeau

HOTEL DROUOT
ADDRESS
9 Rue Drouot, 9th
TELEPHONE
01.48.00.20.20
METRO
Richelieu-Drouot
OPEN
10AM to 6PM, Mon-Sat; exhibitions 10AM to 6PM, day before sale; 10AM to noon, day of sale; auction: 2 to 6PM
Payment in cash in French francs or French check only
$$-$$$$

ADDRESS
18 Avenue Montaigne, 8th
TELEPHONE
01.47.20.75.25
METRO
Alma-Marçeau
OPEN
9:30AM to 6:30PM, Tue-Fri;
9:30AM to 1PM and 2 to
6:30PM, Mon; 9:30AM to 1PM
and 2 to 6PM, Sat
CREDIT CARDS
V, AE, DC
$$$$

3. D. PORTHAULT

Bed, bath, and table linens, children's clothes

Even if you don't spend thousands of dollars on your bed sets, you must visit Porthault simply to educate yourself in the *crème de la crème* of French linens. Like the Princess and the Pea, there are those who reportedly don't leave home without their Porthault, requesting that their beds in the finest hotel rooms be remade before they can properly rest.

Porthault is a prime example of a family business that won't compromise its high standards and original vision. It was the Porthaults who, inspired by the impressionists, introduced the first printed sheets to a society that knew only white embroideries and initials. Since their first designs in 1925, they have also created exclusive motifs for such discerning clients as Jacqueline Onassis, the Duchess of Windsor, and the Shah of Iran, in designs from florals to Greek key motifs. Even the *prêt-à-porter* collection of this house of *couture* linen is woven, dyed, and embroidered to specification.

D. Porthault

If you're prepared to splurge, consider the thickest of terry robes and scalloped toweling, the exquisitely embroidered organdy table linens, and bed linens covered in pink hearts with matching breakfast dishes (the Porthault heart is copied everywhere, but never with the charm of the original). Or just dress up your bed with a double-ruffled boudoir sham cut from the same fabric. A frame to hold nine photos in a distinctively Porthault print can easily be stashed in your suitcase, as can the wood-handled umbrellas that suggest anything but rain. Be sure to peek into the children's area in back to gaze upon exquisite crib and cradle linens for little sleeping beauties, and beautifully smocked children's clothing (newborn to age 10 in dresses, to age 2 in boys clothes). If you're in town in January, don't miss the house sale!

4. CHRISTIAN LACROIX
Women's clothing, shoes, and accessories

It's forever sunny chez Lacroix. No wonder he entered the world of couture in the lead. Fashions here are gay and feminine, inspired by the colorful landscape of his native south of France. The interiors are worth a peek too. Terra-cotta floors, pale yellow walls and roses provide the backdrop for some of the most sought-after designs in Paris. Those who aren't quite prepared to step up to the price tags on his suits and gowns can dress up in costume jewelry that radiates his joie de vivre. For *haute couture*, shop at the boutique on St-Honoré.

ADDRESS
26 Avenue Montaigne, 8th
TELEPHONE
01.47.20.68.95
METRO
Alma-Marçeau

ADDRESS
73 Rue du Faubourg Saint-Honore, 8th
TELEPHONE
01.42.68.79.04
METRO
Champs-Elysées-Clémençeau
OPEN
10AM to 7PM, Mon-Sat
CREDIT CARDS:
V, AE, DC
$$$$

5. CHRISTIAN DIOR
Women's, men's, and children's clothing, accessories, shoes
Women's couture clothing and furs, lingerie, cosmetics, and fragrances
Household linens, accessories, and gifts

The House of Dior is a historic landmark in the world of fashion. M. Dior opened his first small boutique here (the first couture house on the avenue) in 1947, bringing *la mode feminine* (feminine fashion) back to a dreary postwar society with his New Look. The original image of elegant chic, propelled by a visionary business sense, has not faltered, and today the House of Dior is clearly the grande dame of the Avenue. Everything Dior, licensed or made in the couture workshops, is to be found here behind the pearl gray facade. The fabulous interior, completely redone in a neo-18th-century style by architect Peter Marino for the 50th anniversary of the boutique, is a modern marriage of classicism and whimsy.

With the appointment of John Galliano as head couture designer there is a new excitment in the House of Dior. His romantic genius is meant to attract the next generation of stylish clients, and these fitting rooms are already among the busiest on the avenue. His collections can be most affordable if you're in town for the sales at the end of May and November.

ADDRESS
30 Avenue Montaigne, 8th
13 Rue François I (Gift galleries)
11 Bis, Rue François I (Men's boutique)
TELEPHONE
01.40.73.54.44
METRO
Alma-Marçeau
OPEN
10AM to 6:30PM, Mon & Sat;
9:30AM to 6:30PM, Tue-Fri
CREDIT CARDS
V, AE, DC
$$-$$$$

Menswear, newly designed by Patrick Lavoix, has become fresh again, and M. Dior's signature accessory is a silk vest with matching tie.

You may rely on the good taste of Dior for gifts in all price ranges, packaged to perfection. As a testimony to its classicism, I recognize gifts bought during my student days—the same mink-trimmed leather gloves I gave my mother (1200F today) and lavender sweater brought back for my brother, now available in cashmere. This is a must stop for presents that radiate Parisian refinement.

6. PARFUMS CARON
Perfumes

Little-publicized Caron is my favorite perfume house in Paris. Its allure is not only in its sumptuous interior-half a grand chandelier reflected in an antiqued mirror magnifies this small sanctum to magnificence in gilt, glass, and marble. I come here for the re-editions of their perfumes from a bygone era; for their exquisite selection of *flacons* both new and antique (from 450F for something lovely to 4,000F for a limited edition Lalique); for their bath pearls filled with *Nocturnes*, lavender, or champagne perfumes (50F for ten) and my choice of porcelain boxes to hold them; for the hypo-allergenic loose powder in a dozen shades, boxed (200F), and the ostrich powder puff (155F). These items are all musts. If you don't believe me, take your new bath pearls back to the deep tub in your room and have a good soak, perhaps inviting monsieur to share in the lavender?

This is the only Caron boutique in the world, so thank goodness you can reorder your favorites by fax with your credit card. A few of the scents are available in U.S. stores, but most of the 30 or so perfumes and toilet waters are exclusively here, stored in glass urns. The loyal, even lifelong clientele can choose from 18 reissued scents or the famous classics such as *Montaigne*, or the romantic newcomer *Aimez-Moi*. For younger women I would recommend *En Avion*, a 1930 blend of floral and musk.

ADDRESS
34 Avenue Montaigne, 8th
TELEPHONE
01.47.23.40.82
FAX
01.45.63.61.74
METRO
Alma-Marçeau or Franklin D. Roosevelt
OPEN
10AM to 6:30PM, Mon-Sat
CREDIT CARDS
V, AE, MC, DC
$$-$$$$

7. FOUQUET

Candies, condiments, teas, and such

Just a step off the Avenue Montaigne is my favorite
shop for edible gifts. It is here that the Fouquet family
has been busy conjuring up sweets and spices to comfort Parisian palates for four generations—though
today's clientele is international.

Beyond the baskets, boxes, trays, and tins are
shelves lined with all manner of bottles and brown-lid-
ded glass jars filled with distinctively Fouquet jams,
mustards, scented honeys, nuts and fruits, chocolates
and champagnes. Chances are, Christophe Fouquet
will be in the back room conducting experiments for
the sweet tooth that have produced such marvels as
nuts, fruits, or caramels encased in sugar, or a new variety of handmade chocolate. I dare you to make it
home without sampling some of these beautifully displayed goodies.

Perhaps you're better advised to carry back some
of the prepackaged gifts that the Fouquets execute so
famously. Ask them to fill one of their house tins with
the hard candies in fruit or caramel flavors (400-480F a
kilo), and don't overlook the more modest gifts—like
an assortment of their own six mustards, touched with
cognac, shallot, honey, or fine herbs (132F), a jar of
delicately scented honey (30F), or a small jar filled
with chocolate beads to delight the children.

ADDRESS
22 Rue Francois 1, 8th
TELEPHONE
01.47.23.30.36
METRO
Alma-Marçeau or Franklin D.
Roosevelt
OPEN
9:30AM to 7:30PM, Mon-Sat
CREDIT CARDS
V, AE, DC
$$-$$$$

Fouquet

ADDRESS
3 Rue Chambigues, 8th
TELEPHONE
01.47.20.98.24
FAX
01.49.52.05.27
METRO
Alma-Marçeau
OPEN
10AM to 7PM, Mon-Fri; 10 to
6:30, Sat
CREDIT CARDS
V, AE, MC
$$$-$$$$

8. SEPCOEUR
Handbags and belts

These darling little handbags by Margelle Stora have caught the eye of fashionable women around the world, as well as couturiers Yves St-Laurent and Ungaro, who have requested her designs. Ever popular are her colorful evening bags in bright satins and velvets, some quilted and studded with hearts or stars; her refined black satin with a bow; and her ultra-feminine bridal bags. Daytime bags are in leather or lambskin, also designed with whimsy. The accommodating Mme Stora will take orders for next-day delivery or mail to the U.S., will custom color, and can whip up a belt (800 to 2,000F) to coordinate with any bag. Handbags run 1,400 to 2,000F.

Chez Andre

 CHEZ ANDRE
Restaurant

ADDRESS
12 Rue Marbeuf, 8th
TELEPHONE
01.47.20.59.57
METRO
Franklin D. Roosevelt
OPEN
noon to 1PM, every day
CREDIT CARDS
V, AE, MC, DC

When I'm staying in the area, I eat here every day. Somehow the faces always seem familiar, the waitresses seem to know you, and the food is everything you hope for in bourgeois French cuisine. Among the customers I've noticed business people from nearby broadcasting and couture houses, groups of chic singles, families celebrating, older couples, even a gentleman with his lapdog. Make no mistake, this is a popular spot. Full lunches or dinners run about 200f.

9. VIGNON
Gourmet take-out

One of the prettiest of neighborhood take-outs, Vignon is a good address for window-shopping or elegant picnic fare. Enter through the marble facade and choose something delicious to keep in your hotel minibar. Menu choices change daily, and M. Vignon is particularly celebrated for his terrine of *foie gras* and game pâtés.

ADDRESS
14 Rue Marbeuf, 8th
TELEPHONE
01.47.20.24.26
METRO
Franklin Roosevelt
OPEN
8:30AM to 8PM, Mon-Fri, 10AM to 7PM, Sat
CREDIT CARDS
V, AE, MC
$$-$$$

10. NINA RICCI
Women's couture & ready-to-wear, lingerie, accessories, home accessories
Menswear and accessories (at Ricci Club)

If you are familiar with Nina Ricci only as maker of one of the world's best-selling perfumes, *"L'Air du Temps,"* you'll have quite a shock as you walk through the portals of the impressive Avenue Montaigne store. An empire of luxe has grown discreetly from the Ricci couture name established in the 1930s: the oldest couture house still run by its founding family. Couture, now designed by Gerard Pipart, is upstairs, and sophisticated ready-to-wear is on the main floor. On your way there, be sure to stop at costume jewelry, which is traditional and among the best of its kind. The shawls are lovely and varied, and evening accessories, including embroidered footwear, hair ornaments, and bags, are just right for the Ball. The famous lingerie is, of course, exquisite. Downstairs is an entire department of Ricci designs for the home.

The greatest bargain on the street is the boutique tucked around the corner on the rue Francois 1re, given over to half-price-and-lower runway and sample clothing worn by last year's Ricci mannequins, both couture and ready-to-wear. All are in model size 38 (6), but don't despair—they will alter at no extra charge. I once found a floor-length couture evening gown here, something like what the Old Lady in Babar books wears, but entirely hand-beaded, at a price I figured to be less than a quarter of its value. This is what the French call a *bonne affaire.*

ADDRESS
39 Avenue Montaigne, 8th
17 Rue François 1re, 8th (Discounted couture)
19 Rue Francois 1re, 8th (Ricci Club)
TELEPHONE
01.49.52.56.00
METRO
Alma-Marçeau or Franklin-Roosevelt
OPEN
10AM to 6:30PM, Mon-Fri;
10AM to 1PM & 2:15 to 6:30PM, Sat
CREDIT CARDS:
V, AE, MC, DC
$$-$$$$

ADDRESS
38 Rue François Ier, 8th
PHONE
01.47.20.73.13
METRO
Franklin D. Roosevelt
OPEN
10AM to 6:30PM, Mon-Sat
CREDIT CARDS
V, AE, MC
$$-$$$

11. TRENTE-HUIT FRANÇOIS PREMIER
Designer discounts, women's clothing, shoes, and accessories

The discrete entrance, between black and white banners announcing only the address, leads through a garden courtyard to one of the newest and best of the upscale discount shops. Only steps from the couturiers of the Avenue Montaigne, you'll find last year's models from the likes of Lacroix, Dior, Hermès, Valentino, and the rest, at savings of up to 70 percent.

The shop keeps winter and summer seasons in stock year-round, and is expanding to the second floor, so keep your expectations high. In-house alterations are done by an expert in couture.

ADDRESS
40 Rue François I, 8th
TELEPHONE
01.53.67.30.73
METRO
Franklin Roosevelt
OPEN
10AM to 7PM, Mon-Sat
CREDIT CARDS
V, AE, MC
$$$

12. COURRÈGES
Women's clothing

Remember the futuristic fashions of André Courrèges in the late 1960s? They're back, designed by Mme Courrèges in the style of her husband, and they still look like the 21st century. The new boutique coincides with a renewal in the popularity of Courrèges' distinctive concepts: stark white accessories, A-line dresses in candy colors, geometric shapes and lots of shiny plastics. The vinyl jacket (1,200F) and miniskirt (750F) with Courrèges short boots (600F) will look just right on the woman of today.

Next door to the boutique is its CAFE BLANC where the neighborhood stops for a continental breakfast (only 25F), lunch, or a pooped shopper pick-me-up, all served in shiny white surroundings.

Hermès-Motsch

 LA MAISON DU CHOCOLAT

Chocolates, tea salon

ADDRESS
52 Rue Francois I, 8th
TELEPHONE
01.47.23.38.25
METRO
Franklin D. Roosevelt
OPEN
9:30AM to 7:30PM, Mon-Sat

ADDRESS
225 Rue du Faubourg St Honoré, 8th
TELEPHONE
01.42.27.39.44

ADDRESS
8 Boulevard de la Madeleine, 9th
TELEPHONE
01.47.42.86.52

Owner Robert Linxe is the acknowledged master of chocolate in Paris, and perfector of chocolate for the the modern taste that is very rich, less sweet, even a little bitter. The chocolate brown interior and serving help literally enrobed in chocolate will leave you with little desire for anything else, so make your way to the tea salon at the rear of the shop where you can indulge your sweet tooth in any of five unctuous hot chocolates, flagrantly rich pastries, and iced summer specialties. What better pick-me-up for the pooped shopper?

13. HERMÈS-MOTSCH

Men's and women's hats, clothing, and accessories

Probably the most notable men's hatter in Paris (designs for women are less plentiful here), Motsch had been a father-son establishment since 1887 until coming under the management of Mlle Christine Motsch, and was recently sold to Hermès, who now sells a selection of its luxury goods at the same address. Motsch continues to top off numerous heads in France with traditional designs ranging from their bestselling plain felt (all the rage at 1,710F) and Borsolino, to caps, berets, and Panamas, each made from excellent materials and old-world methods exclusively for Motsch. The huge stock, beautifully paneled interior, and expert fitters assure that this stop is worthwhile.

ADDRESS
42 Avenue Georges V, 8th
TELEPHONE
01.47.23.79.22
FAX
01.47.20.59.60
METRO
Georges V
OPEN
10AM to 7PM, Tue-Sat; closed part of August
CREDIT CARDS
V
$$$

ADDRESS
39 Avenue Franklin D.
Roosevelt, 8th
TELEPHONE
01.43.59.77.74
FAX
01.42.56.21.11
METRO
Franklin D. Roosevelt
OPEN
10AM to 7PM, Tue-Sat
CREDIT CARDS
V, AE, MC
$$$$

14. GASTINNE-RENETTE
Men's and women's hunt clothing and gear

This beautiful store has everything for the hunt and is
highly recommended to the armchair hunter as well.
An elegant line of country clothing will tempt even the
gentlest of souls. The standard of craftsmanship with
which Gastinne-Renette armed the csar of Russia and
the king of Spain is now aimed at their hunting rifles
(made downstairs), their leather goods, and the attire.
As expected, activity picks up Friday afternoons, as
couples arrive by station wagon to pick up extras for
the country weekend. A catalog is available.

Along the Way

The Champs-Elysées—no longer the Elysian Fields for which it was named, transforms
from a crowded rush of humanity during the day, to an open-air social club at night.
Walk fast along this still-beautiful avenue to avoid close encounters and beware the
pickpockets. You'll always find a celebrity crowd at LE FOUQUET (N.99), the landmark café-restaurant where a television talk show is filmed nightly. This is a good street
for teen shopping, beginning with LIGHT (N.92), whose racks crammed with clothes
from sleazy to chic beckon from the sidewalk.

ADDRESS
133 Avenue des Champs-
Elysées, 8th
TELEPHONE
01.47.20.94.40
METRO
Etoile
OPEN
9 to 2AM, daily

ADDRESS
1 Avenue Matignon, 8th
TELEPHONE
01.43.59.38.70
METRO
Franklin D. Roosevelt
OPEN
9 to 2AM, daily
CREDIT CARDS
V, AE, MC, DC
$$-$$$

15. DRUGSTORE PUBLICIS
Restaurant, pharmacy, books and magazines, food, gifts

When the first 'Drugstore' opened on the Champs-
Elysées, curious Frenchmen and homesick Americans
came in droves for the burgers, fries, and ice cream
sundaes, and its boutiques offered a destination for
night owls prowling the Champs. Now a Drugstore
exists at both ends of the avenue, giving everyone so
inclined an excuse to roam back and forth 'til the wee
hours.

If you're stuck with last minute gift needs or a late
craving for a good read in English, come here to find
anything from toys and cigars to travel bags. No food
or reading materials at Matignon location.

16. J. M. WESTON
Men's and women's shoes

When a certain class of Frenchman sizes you up, he looks first at your shoes, and if they happen to be Westons he'll rest assured you are well heeled. The Weston shoe is a status symbol among the executive set, and to affluent teens, who save up for a conservative Weston as an American would for Air Jordans. The heavy leather shoes, classically styled, are pure quality. The famous Weston moccasin runs 1,600F, and the golf shoe is considered the best in the world (from 2,250F). There is even an additional strip of leather where the sole meets the top of the shoe to prevent leaks. At those prices, you should hope they will never wear out!

ADDRESS
114 Avenue des Champs-Elysées, 8th
TELEPHONE
01.45.62.26.47
METRO
Georges V
OPEN
9:30AM to 7PM, Tue-Sat; 10AM to 7PM, Mon

ADDRESS
3 Boulevard de la Madeleine, 1st
TELEPHONE
01.42.61.11.87
METRO
Madeleine
OPEN
2 to7PM, Mon; 10AM to 7PM, Tue-Sat

ADDRESS
49 Rue de Rennes, 6th
TELEPHONE
01.45.49.38.50
METRO
St-Sulpice
OPEN
2:30 to 7PM, Mon; 10AM to 7PM, Tue-Sat

ADDRESS
97 Avenue Victor-Hugo, 16th
TELEPHONE
01.47.04.23.75
METRO
Victor-Hugo
OPEN
2 to 7PM, Mon; 10AM to 7PM, Tue-Sat
CREDIT CARDS
V
$$$-$$$$

ADDRESS
70, Avenue des Champs-
Elysées, 8th
TELEPHONE
01.53.93.22.50
METRO
Franklin D. Roosevelt
OPEN
10AM to midnight, Mon-Sat;
Noon to 9PM, Sunday

ADDRESS
50 Rue de Passy, 16th
TELEPHONE
01.45.20.03.15
METRO
Muette
OPEN
9:30AM to 7:30PM, Mon-Sat
CREDIT CARDS
V, AE, MC
$$

17. SEPHORA
Perfumes and Cosmetics

Enter the twilight zone when you enter here.
www.sephora.com's new flagship store on the Champs-
Elysées is a cutting edge makeover for the perfume and
cosmetics warehouse known for its universal inventory
and cut-rate prices. Everything about this enormous
space is futuristic, from the young salesgirls in long
black robes and gloves, to the wordless, haunting
music that never stops.

It's a virtual world unto itself where you'll find vir-
tually any brand you're seeking, many at a savings of
about 20 percent. If you're working toward the all-day
face, don't miss the special room where you can test
your makeup under lighting conditions from day to
night.

If the world described above isn't for you, try the
more exclusive GUERLAIN, next door at N. 68, with
its luxurious art deco interior. Guerlain fragrances are
pure French sophistication and only available at the
Guerlain boutiques in France. Ask to try those that are
not available in the U.S. Also at this address is a highly
recommended Guerlain skin treatment center.

ADDRESS
52-60 Avenue des Champs-
Elysées, 8th
TELEPHONE
01.40.74.06.48
METRO
Franklin D. Roosevelt
OPEN
10AM to midnight, Mon-Thurs;
10AM to 1PM, Fri & Sat; noon to
midnight, Sun
CREDIT CARDS
V, AE, DC
$$

18. THE VIRGIN MEGASTORE
Musical recordings, books, electronics

An English import (an offshoot of the Virgin Record
label) this is the biggest record store in France, and a
destination attraction on the Champs-Elysées. On a
restless night it's a place to see and be seen.

Three floors and 35,000 square feet are a *palais* of
high-tech design and technology, with headphones for
sampling recordings from the international musical
scene. Some top names in French rock 'n' roll are
Ophélie Winter and M. C. Solaar. Not in the past
noted for this particular genre of music, but never to
be culturally outdone, the French have instituted the
post of Minister of Pop Music, with a big budget for
finding and promoting local talent. A new law requires
French radio to play 60 percent French music.

You'll find every kind of music here, on record,
cassette, or CD, as well as an excellent selection of
books. For a mid-browse pick-me-up, find a spot
upstairs at the VIRGIN CAFE.

Along the Way

The lovely AVENUE MATIGNON is a prime location for high-priced but priceless art and antique galleries. Poke around the stamp and old post card collectors' market held here and down the AVENUE GABRIEL on Thursdays, Saturdays, Sundays, and holidays from 10AM to sunset.

Continue down to the CARRE MARIGNY (corner of Avenues Marigny and Gabriel) to the stamp market where licensed dealers buy, sell, and trade philatelia from booths set up on the sidewalks, keeping the same hours as above.

19. ARTCURIAL
Art, art books, jewelry

Enter through the portals of this well-established haven for art lovers and you'll step into a large and lively gallery of contemporary art and handmade jewelry on the main floor. Upstairs is the city's second-largest collection of books on the arts (over 8,000 volumes here; the art bookshop in the Louvre Museum claims to be the largest in the world). Find lots of modern prints here too.

ADDRESS
9 Avenue Matignon, 8th
TELEPHONE
01.42.99.16.16
METRO
Franklin D. Roosevelt
OPEN
10:30AM to 7:15PM, Tue-Sat and Mon in December; closed first 3 weeks in August
CREDIT CARDS
V, AE, DC
$$$-$$$$

20. ANNA LOWE
Discount women's clothing

Anna's is one of the better discount shops in Paris because here they are service-oriented even when offering the big names in couture at around 40 percent off. Many of the couture and *haute couture* models for day and evening come in right after the runway shows, so you can buy for the current season. During one visit I noticed a red Chanel suit in the window, offered at 9,250F, that was still available for 15,200F at the Chanel boutique down the street! Tags are marked with the original and discounted prices and you'll be helped in English with *détaxe* and alterations, of course.

ADDRESS
104 Rue du Faubourg St-Honoré, 8th
TELEPHONE
01.42.66.11.32
METRO
Madeleine
OPEN
10:30AM to 7PM, Mon-Sat
CREDIT CARDS
V, AE, DC
$$-$$$

ADDRESS
24 Rue du Faubourg St-
Honoré, 8th
TELEPHONE
01.40.17.47.17
FAX
01.40.17.47.18
METRO
Concorde
OPEN
10AM to 6:30PM, Mon-Sat

ADDRESS
42 Avenue Georges V
(Hermès-Motsch)
TELEPHONE
01.47.20.48.51
METRO
Georges V
OPEN
10AM to 7:30PM, Mon-Sat
CREDIT CARDS
V, AE, DC
$$$-$$$$

October sale at Hermès

21. HERMÈS

Everyone knows the name Hermès, but you don't real-
ly know Hermès until you've visited this landmark
store. Our present-day fascination with the elegant
country, horsey life has no better interpreter than the
window and interior designers here, and all of Paris
knows it. Crowds come just to take in the autumn
scenes from the sidewalk, while inside customers jam
the aisles. At one time considered stodgy, the Hermès
look has been revitalized for a younger generation of
trend setters. Once again the scarf counter is mobbed
with chic young things who leave with their status-
symbol silk twill (over 200 different styles, averaging
1,390F) and the little booklet that shows just how to
tie it.

The incomparable leather clothing is classically
styled with the freshest of colors. And the Kelly bag
(carried by Princess Grace to Monaco for her wed-
ding) has been the best-selling handbag in the world,
with a customer waiting list of 18 months.

The success of Hermès, which began as a saddlery
in 1837, and its recent growth (the workshops just
moved from this location to the outskirts of Paris to
make room for more selling space), are thanks to the
recognition of a new crop of customers appreciative of
the first-rate craftsmanship in every Hermès product.
Handbags, for example, are made by hand and guaran-
teed for life.

Those willing to pay Hermès prices will be thrilled
not just with the image but with the perfect product.
Leather connoisseurs note that Hermès skins always
have a pleasant odor because the otherwise acceptable
hide will be rejected if not up to the proper snuff. The
useful small leather items are big sellers with relatively
small price tags, and so are the distinctively Hermès
men's neckties (from 580F). If you just can't get enough
of the look, ask to visit the upstairs museum.

The Hermès sales, held in mid-October and mid-
March for a week, have customers lined up around the
block and around the clock, just waiting their turn to
enter the back rooms. Prices are about 40 percent off,
and more.

At Hermès-Motsch, you'll find a small collection
of Hermès basics alongside the Motsch hat collection.

22. RENAUD PELLEGRINO
Handbags

Pellegrino bags are like pieces of modern art, and among the most artful in Paris. For to M Pellegrino, a handbag is to be worn as jewelry, not as a mere tote. Thus his elegant designs come in compact, original shapes, often with whimsically molded handles, and in five sizes and many colors. The leather bags are quite costly, coming from the same skins as Hermès, including the lizard and ostrich; but the extraordinary satin evening bags, whether studded with semiprecious-looking stones or simply with a clear crystal necklace as a handle, are a real value (from 1,500F).

If you carry only a lipstick, keys, and phone money to your dressy *soirées*, why not indulge in something stunning? There are also a number of very pretty belts, leather goods, and silk scarves.

ADDRESS
14 Rue du Faubourg St-Honoré, 8th (In the courtyard)
TELEPHONE
01.42.65.35.52
METRO
Concorde
OPEN
10AM to 7PM, Mon-Sat
CREDIT CARDS
V, AE, MC
$$$-$$$$

Renaud Pellegrino

23. L. B. D. LOFT
Women's and men's clothing

Good buys on well-styled men's, women's, and unisex clothing abound in this high-tech loft. Comfortable, relatively tame designs for the urban jungle are available here in dark city colors that lend themselves to mixing and matching. Here's where to put together an office ensemble that can be altered on-the-spot. Even the sweats are distinctive.

ADDRESS
12 Rue du Faubourg St-Honoré, 8th
TELEPHONE
01.42.65.59.65
METRO
Concorde or Madeleine

ADDRESS
56 Rue de Rennes, 6th
TELEPHONE
01.45.44.88.99
METRO
St-Germaine des Prés
OPEN
10AM to 7PM, Mon-Sat
CREDIT CARDS
V, AE, MC, DC
$$

Couture Along the Way

The RUE DU FAUBOURG ST-HONORE is the best-known shopping street in Paris for good reason: it is lined with fine shops and many couture designers have *prêt-à-porter* boutiques here. Beginning across the street from the ELYSÉES PALACE (home of the French President) it's easy to spend a day going into every store down the Faubourg and its continuation, the Rue St-Honoré, or simply enjoying the window displays. English is spoken everywhere, and the *détaxe* and credit cards are no problem.

Among the many couture names to watch for on St-Honoré are LOUIS FERAUD (N.88 & 90), who designs alluring clothes that even a first lady can wear, as orders from the Palace across the street have proven; CHRISTIAN LACROIX (N.73), whose fantasies have brought his native south-of-France sunlight back into fashion; YVES ST LAURENT (N.38) and YSL ACCESSORIES (N.32) for his shoes, costume jewelry, belts, bags, and scarves; LANVIN (N.22) for elegant pieces in keeping with the style of Jeanne Lanvin, including accessories and moderately priced costume jewelry designed for her house in the '20s; KARL LAGERFELD (N.17) who designs his own line of *prêt-à-porter* in addition to his designs for Chanel, and whose signature outfits are taking the place of Chanel in the armoires of many a Parisienne (and yes, they are a bit less).

ADDRESS
11 Rue du Faubourg St-Honoré, 8th
TELEPHONE
01.42.65.79.00
METRO
Concorde or Madeleine

CARITA MONTAIGNE
ADDRESS
3 Rue du Boccador
TELEPHONE
01.47.23.76.76
OPEN
9AM to 7PM, Mon-Fri
CREDIT CARDS
V, AE, MC
$$$

24. INSTITUT CARITA
Beauty salon

The Carita sisters, Rosy and Maria, were the first to offer treatments for skin, body and hair together, creating the concept of the beauty institute. The St-Honoré Carita location is now the largest temple of beauty in Paris, known for its premier quality treatments, ultra-stylish coifs and celebrity clientele.

A beauty break in the luxury of this feminine salon is designed to tranquilize the nervous '90s. Make an appointment for your hair, a classic facial, French manicure, makeup, massage, or come for a *jour de beauté* (day of beauty), and leave feeling completely pampered. Before you go, check the excellent selection of hair accessories. It's always busy here; the *Parisienne* visits her salon weekly.

25. FAÇONNABLE

A great place to find the American casual wear look with a European flair, Façonnable is otherwise described by an elegant American friend in Paris as "a French version of Ralph Lauren." Even if the rest of French sartorial style won't do for him, he'll surely be delighted with Façonnable.

Men's sportswear is designed with American comfort and French color consciousness in mind. French-cuffed corduroy shirts come in every hue from salmon to black and discreetly branded with the house logo (a bird holding a golf club, at 575F). Visit upstairs for outerwear, including a few fashionable concessions to that rarity, the true sportsman.

While he's marveling at the hundreds of very wide ties (from 350F) and suspenders in every possible combination, surprise him with a pair of irresistible *caleáons* (boxer shorts) in mixed florals or patchwork checks (from 195F).

ADDRESS
9 Rue du Faubourg St-Honoré, 8th
TELEPHONE
01.47.42.72.60
METRO
Concorde

ADDRESS
174 Boulevard St-Germain, 6th
TELEPHONE
01.40.49.02.47
METRO
St-Germain-des-Prés
OPEN
10AM to 7PM, Mon-Sat
CREDIT CARDS
V, AE, DC
$$$

Casoar

26. CASOAR
Jewelry and decorative items in silver

When Mme Casoar opened her shop 10 years ago, I would come here for her period designs in silverplate. Today her fantasies are realized in solid silver. The finely molded picture frames, jewelry, and perfume flasks are inspired by the styles of the art deco and Napoleonic periods and are made to last forever. But the store decor is always a surprise, as Madame redesigns the stylish interior monthly, carting the large furnishings back and forth from her country *château*. It is always a pleasure to enter here, particularly knowing you can pick up a sparkling beetle or firefly to pin to your scarf for 360F, or an enamel silver Empire frame from 700 to 7,000F.

ADDRESS
15 Rue Boissy d'Anglas, 8th
TELEPHONE
01.47.42.69.51
FAX
01.40.07.04.17
METRO
Concorde
OPEN
2:30 to 5PM, Mon; 10:30AM to 1:30PM and 2:30 to 5PM, Tue-Sat
CREDIT CARDS
V, AE
$$-$$$

Along the Way

The RUE ROYALE, leading up to the CHURCH OF LA MADELEINE, is where the rich and royal traditionally window shopped on the way to the restaurant MAXIME'S (N.3 Rue Royale), whose magnificent *belle époque* interior still draws a crowd despite inconsistent meals and high prices. On this showcase street are some of the grandest names in French tableware. You'll pass BERNARDAUD LIMOGES (N.11 Rue Royale), France's whitest and bestselling porcelain,whose lovely tea salon is tucked away in the pedestrian passage Galérie Royale (N.9 Rue Royale); CRISTALLERIES DE ST-LOUIS (N.13 Rue Royale), whose weighty hand-cut crystal dates back to royal tables of the 1700s; ODIOT (N.7 Place de la Madeleine), where pieces in gold, silver and

Rue Royale

vermeil are cast in 18th- and 19th-century molds; BACCARAT (N.11 Place de la Madeleine), whose flagship store shows off this delicate crystal in a luxurious setting at prices up to 30 percent under U.S. retail, after shipping costs. At N. 25 you'll find the entrance to the VILLAGE ROYALE, at first glance a 17th-century village street, very well preserved; actually a shopping mall redo of the royal barracks of that era.

ADDRESS
9 Rue Royale, 8th
TELEPHONE
01.49.33.43.00
METRO
Madeleine
OPEN
10AM to 7PM, Mon-Sat
CREDIT CARDS
V, AE, DC
$$$

27. PAVILLON CHRISTOFLE
Silver and table arts

The dazzling Christofle pavilion illustrates the fine French art of setting a beautiful table, and is one of the best addresses in the city for gifts. You'll find a wealth of beautiful, packable objects that simply ooze good taste, suited to a range of purposes (office, jewelry, entertaining) and prices.

A celebrated silversmith from the days when the haute bourgeoisie would dine with nothing less, Christofle has added an extensive selection of silver-plated flatware as well as the real thing in designs from baroque to stark.

Go downstairs for tables set with an inspired mix of the major French table brands (Baccarat, Limoges, and the rest are also for sale here) including porcelain made for Christofle. The shops are all set up for shipping treasures to America. Choose an adorable silver animal figurine (from 320F), a Louis XI bottle opener (250F), or a dozen silver dinner settings. Ask for a catalog for further orders.

28. LALIQUE
Crystal and table arts

Even if you've never longed for Lalique, you should
take a peek at its crystal kingdom. From doorknob to
chandelier, the Lalique touch glistens. Since René
Lalique changed the face of glassware with his large
deco-influenced sculptures at the turn of the century,
Lalique has added facets to the range of the medium.
Now working primarily in crystal, and specializing in a
marriage of clear and frosted glass, Marie-Claude
Lalique is charged with assuring her family name is
present in the gift bags of presidents and kings
(Lalique is a typical gift from the French president to
another head of state) as well as their countrymen.

For innovative wearable crystal, see the belt buck-
les, stickpins and the rings in 15 different colors and
10 finger sizes. If you are a fan of Lalique, the selection
of figurines, vases, and tableware is at its best here, and
prices are 30 percent less than in the U.S., with a further *detaxe* that's close to the price of shipping.
Continue through the courtyard to their new table arts
boutique.

ADDRESS
11 Rue Royale, 8th
TELEPHONE
01.53.05.12.12
METRO
Concorde
OPEN
10AM to 6:30PM, Mon; 9:30AM
to 6:30PM, Tue-Fri; 9:30AM to
7PM, Sat
CREDIT CARDS
V, AE, MC, DC
$$$

Christofle

LADUREE
Tea salon

ADDRESS
16 Rue Royale, 8th
TELEPHONE
01.42.60.21.79
METRO
Madeleine

ADDRESS
75 Avenue des Champs-Elysées, 8th
TELEPHONE
01.40.75.08.75
METRO
Georges V
OPEN
8:30AM to 7PM, Mon-Sat; closed August

This is my favorite tea salon, and I'm among its many ardent fans. Some love it for its morning café crème and flaky croissant; some claim it has the richest hot chocolate in the city; others rapture over the tea sandwich menu (18 varieties from 11 to 14F). But I come here for the cherub-frescoed ceiling, and the chocolate macaroon which is second to none.

At the recently opened Champs-Elysées salon, whose interior is inspired by the ironwork designs of Gustave Eiffel, the proprietors appropriately repeat the legendary menu.

ADDRESS
15 Place de la Madeleine, 8th
METRO
Madeleine
OPEN
12:30 to 8PM, Tue-Fri; 12:30 to 2PM (matinee tickets only) and 2 to 8PM (evening performances), Sat; 12:30 to 6PM, Sun
NO CREDIT CARDS

29. KIOSQUE THÉÂTRE
Discounted tickets to theaters and special events

Same-day ticket sales for some of the best (leftover) seats in the house. Theater, dance, circuses, you name it. This last-minute commitment is an easy way for the harried traveler to partake of Parisian nightlife. And prices drop more than 50 percent off earlier ticket prices (plus a 13 percent commission). As the Saturday lineup can be quite long, I recommend you arrive early that day.

30. FAUCHON
Grocery, pastries, restaurant, take-out

No one who enjoys food will want to miss Fauchon, France's great homage to the glory of grocery shopping. From a tiny greengrocer stand in 1866, Fauchon has gained landmark status for its showstopping displays of over 20,000 food items.

From fresh exotic fruits to fish and take-out mini-Fauchon (N.26), make your way to the bustling pastry and candy shop (N.28), and on to the tabletop and packaged foods hall (N.30), where accommodating salespeople can turn even the tiniest offering (perhaps an ingenious 5F tube of sweet chestnut cream for home-baked goodies) into a coveted treat packaged *à la Fauchon* while you take your receipt to the cashier.

Fauchon is the ultimate in quick-picks for food items to send or carry home, if you can navigate the crowds, because you'll find everything from wine and pâté to Far-Eastern condiments, prepackaged to carry or ship.

Since its recent expansion you needn't content yourself with drooling at the windows. The cafeteria-bar-tea salon in the basement of N.30 offers self-service Fauchon quality eats, and there's an epicurean restaurant upstairs that is open for dinner. I highly recommend a stand-up lunch in the pastry shop.

ADDRESS
26,28,30 Place de la Madeleine, 8th
TELEPHONE
01.47.42.60.11
FAX
01.47.42.83.75
METRO
Madeleine
OPEN
9:40AM to 7PM, Mon-Sat; mini-Fauchon open to 8:30PM
CREDIT CARDS
V, AE, DC
$$-$$$$

Fauchon

ADDRESS
34 Rue Tronchet, 8th
TELEPHONE
01.47.42.12.61
METRO
Havre-Caumartin

ADDRESS
6 Rue Bonaparte, 6th
TELEPHONE
01.40.46.00.45
METRO
St-Germain-des-Prés

ADDRESS
5 Place des Victoires, 1st
(Women's only)
TELEPHONE
01.42.33.29.88
METRO
Etienne-Marcel or Palais-Royal
OPEN
10:15AM to 7PM, Mon-Sat
CREDIT CARDS
V, AE

CACHAREL STOCK (DISCOUNT)
ADDRESS
114 Rue d'Alésia, 14th
TELEPHONE
01.45.42.53.04
METRO
Alésia
OPEN
10AM to 7PM, Tue-Sat; 2 to
7PM, Mon
CREDIT CARDS
V
$$-$$$$

ADDRESS
11 Rue Vignon, 8th
TELEPHONE
01.47.42.25.93
METRO
Madeleine
OPEN
10AM to 7:00PM, Mon-Sat
CREDIT CARDS
V
$$-$$$

31. CACHAREL
Women's, men's, children's clothing, layette

Cacharel offers much more than the flowered blouses and shirts that once made their name. Their updated image is contemporary and still refined. A new Cacharel shop is opening at 64 Rue Bonaparte, 6th, that will inaugurate the look of simple sophistication. Meanwhile,the shop on the Rue Tronchet is an easy family stop for an immensely wearable, decently made, well-priced wardrobe for everyone, and the ambiance feels as fresh as the collection, quite in contrast to the mad crush at the nearby department stores.

While the colorful cotton shirts for men and women are back in style, and take up the entire main floor, you'll find a clean look in everything from sweater sets to sunglasses in women's wear upstairs. Children's fashions (these kids' classics are cut small, so buy large) are on one and men's are through the side entrance.

If you care less about the newest designs and the perfect ambiance, try Cacharel Stock for last year's designs at discounts of 30 yo 40 percent, such as a Liberty print blouse for 220F or a good wool suit for him at 1,525F.

32. LAFONT ET FILS
Eyewear

For three generations the *famille* Lafont has designed and sold eye-catching frames from this old-fashioned interior whose wares are always in tune with the times. Whether your look is strict or whacky, Lafont has it, and he can deliver with your prescription (don't worry, these are international) within 48 hours.

This is Paris, and the establishment will custom style to your measure, color, and shape, upon request.

BABY-SITTING SERVICES

ADDRESS
18 Rue Tronchet, 8th
TELEPHONE
01.46.37.51.24
METRO
Havre-Caumartin
OPEN
7AM to 11:30PM, daily
NO CREDIT CARDS

Within an hour the agency will rush to your hotel room a competent young woman to watch the children while you have a romantic dinner elsewhere. Ask for a sitter who speaks English. Charges are 30F an hour with a 60F agency fee.

33. CHANEL
Women's clothes, accessories, makeup

I once read that a vast majority of French women polled said that if they won the lottery, they would run out to buy a Chanel suit. If you are so lucky, you'll find the best service at the Rue Cambon store, right underneath Coco Chanel's apartment, which two decades after her death is as intact as the Chanel couture name.

Designer Karl Lagerfeld has revitalized the Chanel line with witty takeoffs on Mlle Chanel's innovations like the little black dress, costume jewelry, pants, and short hair for ladies, easy-to-wear jerseys, Chanel N.5—in short, much of what we take for granted in fashions today.

Both shops are typically crowded, and the Rue Cambon store has moved its makeup and costume jewelry down the staircase in the rear of the store. Even if you haven't won the lottery, make your way downstairs for a pair of classic baroque pearl earrings in a braided gold setting (about 1,000F), or a lipstick, perfume, and a makeup demonstration.

If you do decide on a suit, you'll find it as comfortable as a second skin, it won't become outdated, and as they will tell you in the boutique, "After you have worn this one, Madame, you'll be back every year for another."

ADDRESS
31 Rue Cambon, 1st
TELEPHONE
01.42.86.28.00
METRO
Concorde
OPEN
9:30AM to 6:30PM, Mon-Sat

ADDRESS
40 Avenue Montaigne, 8th
(Watches)
TELEPHONE
01.40.70.12.33

ADDRESS
42 Avenue Montaigne, 8th
TELEPHONE
01.47.23.74.12
METRO
Alma-Marçeau
OPEN
9:30AM to 6:30PM, Mon-Fri;
10AM to 1PM & 2 to 6:30PM, Sat
CREDIT CARDS
V, AE, MC
$$$-$$$$

ADDRESS
408 Rue St-Honoré, 8th
TELEPHONE
01.42.60.39.01
METRO
Madeleine or Concorde
OPEN
9:45AM to 6:15PM, Mon-Sat
CREDIT CARDS
V, AE, MC
$-$$$$

34. AU NAIN BLEU

Toys

To a Parisian of a certain size, nothing can compare with the thrill of being offered a package wrapped in the distinctive paper of Au Nain Bleu! One of the world's top toy stores, it has been run by the same family for five generations and attracts a celebrity clientele and children of all ages. Its original exquisite porcelain-faced dolls have grown into a large collection of beautifully dressed mesdemoiselles, some in French folk costumes.

Today, a child can find the world's most popular toys here, but you'll probably want to look beyond the Beanie Babies and wedding Barbies to more typically French items, like knight and Pierrot costumes, toy soldiers (258F for a turned-out Napoleon), marionettes and lots of inventive, inexpensive gadgets that children find so appealing.

For the mademoiselle who has everything, the store has designed an elaborate nursery kit complete with cribs, strollers, changing tables, and babies with their nannies (2,000F range). There are tea sets with wine glasses, napkins, and plates patterned after Maman's Porthault (up to 3,000F) side by side with porcelain tea sets that would fit on a quarter for just a few francs.

Boys on their way to play in the Luxembourg or Tuileries gardens will want a Nain Bleu carrying case of 23 metal vehicles for land, air, and sea (720F) or an inexpensive wooden sailboat, neither of which needs a translator. Happily, Au Nain Bleu ships internationally.

Au Nain Bleu

35. LONGCHAMPS
Luggage, purses, small leather goods

With all the fashion-conscious handbags to choose
from in Paris, I come to Longchamps for my classic,
functional day-bags. The price-to-quality ratio is excellent in these detailed yet sturdy pieces in leather,
nylon or canvas, with every bag made to last like a
piece of luggage.

While young mothers might be drawn to a leather-
cornered nylon zip bag that looks more structured
than the luggage it's made to be, and perfectly
designed for stuffing with leaky baby bottles (it's rub-
berized), camera, and diapers (445F), I now go for the
grainy leather drawstring sac—a sophisticated, well-
detailed bag that still looks good and fetches compliments after a year of use. The briefcases are a smart
buy, and there's a stylish selection of gloves and belts,
as well as lots of small leather goods.

ADDRESS
390 Rue St-Honoré, 1st
TELEPHONE
01.42.60.00.00
METRO
Madeleine

ADDRESS
21 Rue du Vieux-Colombier,
6th
TELEPHONE
01.42.22.74.75
METRO
St-Sulpice
OPEN
10AM to 7PM, Mon-Sat
CREDIT CARDS
V, AE
$$-$$$

36. PIERRE BARBOZA
Antique jewelry

The exterior is quite ordinary, but the antique jewels
inside are of excellent quality and at reasonable prices;
this makes for an unbeatable combination. In the esti-
mation of my French friends who have long relied on
the honesty and good taste of the owners, you may tell
M. and Mme Gribe (the daughter of the original
Barboza) in English what you want and depend on
them to find it for you. The specialty here is 19th and
18th-century jewelry from 300F to 30,000F, and the
shop is known for restyling tired looks like no one
else.

ADDRESS
356 Rue St-Honoré, 1st
TELEPHONE
01.42.60.67.08
METRO
Tuileries
OPEN
10AM to 6PM, Mon-Fri; 10AM to
6PM, Sat in November and
December only
CREDIT CARDS
V, AE
$$-$$$

37. ALEXANDRE DE PARIS
Hair ornaments

ADDRESS
235 Rue St-Honoré, 1st
TELEPHONE
01.42.61.41.34
METRO
Tuileries
OPEN
10AM to 7PM, Mon-Sat
CREDIT CARDS
V, AE
$$$

If you're looking for something to decorate your locks that's a bit more extraordinary than the department store offerings, you'll be overwhelmed with the three floors of bands, barrettes, bows, and combs at Alexandre. These "jewels for the hair" as they're called here, are all handmade in France and Italy exclusively for Alexandre. The finest are embroidered by renowned Lesage, with the simplest velvet or raw silk bands from about 400F.

Take the spiral staircase in back to the third-floor bridal selection of bows, roses, and exquisitely veiled head pieces all in white. If the choices at Alexandre don't fit your lifestyle, head for your corner *Parfumerie* (perfume and cosmetics store) or for the large selection downstairs at GALERIES LAFAYETTES.

38. GOYARD
Leather goods and luggage

ADDRESS
233 Rue St-Honoré, 1st
TELEPHONE
01.42.60.57.04
METRO
Tuilleries
OPEN
10AM to 6:30PM, Mon-Sat
CREDIT CARDS
V, AE, MC
$$$$

One of the city's oldest and most exclusive addresses for luggage, Goyard is where to come when your own initials are enough. A family-run business since 1853, fifth-generation owner Isabelle Goyard continues to offer a luxurious collection of leather luggage, with the addition of a line in plastified canvas in their trademark design of gray and gold herringbone. The leather desk accessories, handbags, and toiletry bags are classics, and the dog collars (from 180F) are just the thing for the pooch who has everything.

Goyard

☕ LA FERME ST-HUBERT

Cheeses, restaurant

ADDRESS
21 Rue Vignon, 8th
TELEPHONE
01.47.42.79.20
METRO
Madeleine
OPEN
9AM to 7:30PM, Mon;
9AM to 9PM, Tue-Sat
(store); 11:45AM to
3:30PM and 7 to 11PM,
Thurs-Sat (restaurant)
CREDIT CARDS
V, DC
$$

La Ferme St-Hubert cheeses

You can count on master cheesemaker Henry Voy to bring the best farmhouse cheeses of France to his immaculate small shop and tend them to perfection in his cellar for an appreciative clientele. The selection involves over 150 different types, so you may want to take a seat in the adjoining restaurant for a quick *dégustation* (perhaps a plate of 7 cheeses with Poilâne bread, washed down with a *Côtes-du-Rhône*) before deciding. Once you know your preference, the French farm life will be easy to recreate at home as the establishment will package cheese for travel (remember that unpasteurized cheeses are not allowed entry into the U.S.). A fromage fanatic will find fulfillment in the restaurant menu, which offers cheese-filled dishes from fondue and raclette to roquefort tortes.

39. CATHERINE

Discount perfumes and cosmetics

ADDRESS
6 Rue de Castiglione, 1st
TELEPHONE
01.42.61.02.87
FAX
01.42.61.02.35
METRO
Tuileries
OPEN
9:30AM to 7:30PM, Mon-Sat
CREDIT CARDS
V, AE, MC
$$

From the outside you'd never guess that Catherine has among the largest stock in town of the perfumes and cosmetics that no tourist can leave without. The trick is in the revolving-shelf wall that the salesgirl will put into action when you give her your order. Most major scents are offered here (Guerlain, Goutal, and Caron are exceptions) as well as beauty products for 25 percent off French retail (before *détaxe*) and up to 45 percent for purchases of 1,200F.

Shopping is made easy for Americans here, and you can request to be on the mailing list to continue ordering at these low prices from home and pay in dollars.

☕ HÔTEL RITZ
HÔTEL RITZ TEA SALON
RITZ-ESCOFFIER COOKING SCHOOL

ADDRESS
15 Place Vendôme, 1st
TELEPHONE
01.42.60.38.30
METRO
Concorde
CREDIT CARDS
V, AE, MC

This beautiful hotel is still considered to be foremost in the world for its fine service among those who are fortunate enough to stay here, and it is an experience within reach at teatime. The three-course English Tea in the salon (195F) or a cocktail on the terrace are a welcome respite for the stressed shopper. Gentlemen, a necktie is *de rigueur*.

You will want to reserve at least one day ahead (1-800-966-5758 from the U.S.) for a cooking demonstration/tasting class by the chefs at the exceptional Ritz-Escoffier Cooking School. Classes are 3PM to 5:30PM, Mon, Tue and Thurs; 7 to 9:30PM, first Tue of every month. Cost is 275F per session or 1,375F for 6 sessions. Entrance to the school is at 38 Rue Cambon. Be sure to pick up information about the full range of cooking programs available.

While you're here, don't miss the shopping gallery down the wing to the right of the main hotel entrance, where display cases present a sampling from many nearby boutiques.

Along the Way

On the PLACE VENDOME is the HÔTEL RITZ, whose parking lot is built under the cobblestones originally laid for the carriages of Louis XIV. Surrounding this bastion of luxury is a glittering array of fine jewelry houses: MORABITO, N.1; CARTIER, N.7; CHANEL, N.7; CHAUMET, N.12; MAUBOUSSIN, N.20; VAN CLEEF & ARPELS, N.22; ALEXANDRE REZA, N.23; BUCHERON, N.26. A well-kept secret among less conventional Parisians is JARS, upstairs in N.7, where American Joel A. Rosenthal works magic with gold and stones.

40. CHARVET
Men's shirts, neckwear, suits, women's shirts

ADDRESS
28 Place Vendôme, 1st
TELEPHONE
01.42.60.30.70
FAX
01.42.96.27.07
METRO
Opéra
OPEN
9:45AM to 6:30PM, Mon-Sat
CREDIT CARDS
V, AE
$$$-$$$$

The gentlemanly tradition is in good form at Charvet, where meticulous souls as diverse as Proust, Chanel, and de Gaulle have been coming for tailored clothing since 1838. The philosophy here, to offer the greatest choice possible, may send you reeling if you don't enlist the counsel of the well-trained staff. The 1,000 *prêt-à-porter* models (from 950F) with 50 collars and 15 cuff styles may be worn with your choice of hundreds of necktie designs, each available in 20 to 60 color-ways (510F). The array is astounding and the standards are the highest.

Even the shirts are made one-by-one and are proudly touted to be as beautiful inside as out. If you opt for a custom shirt (no minimum) the tailors will have you choose from their 6,000 rolls of the finest shirting cottons and take no fewer than 25 measurements, requiring one fitting the following week (from 1,250F). Your particulars will be kept in copious client files (no computers here!) and in the future you may request fabric samples and place orders by mail.

For women, shirts come in three sizes, 60 colors, and many models (950F), including silks in styles Chanel herself wore.

For an elegant gift for a man, you can't go wrong with the trademark braided-knot cuff links (165F for three pairs in a suede pouch, any colors) to versions in gold and silver. Charvet neckwear now rivals Hermès as a symbol of status at a lower price. There are suede slippers ready-to-travel in a bag; and the house blend of silk and cashmere is fashioned into scarves, polos, and robes.

Charvet windows

Charvet shoes

ADDRESS
22 Rue de la Paix, 2nd
TELEPHONE
01.44.71.83.22
METRO
Opéra
HOURS
10AM to 7PM, Mon-Sat (store);
9AM to 6PM, Mon-Sat (custom
workshop)
CREDIT CARDS
V
$$

41. REPETTO
Dancewear

Ballerinas from all over Paris, from prima ballerinas and
les petits rats (youngest ballerinas) of the nearby Opéra
Garnier, to Angelina mouse-size preschoolers, come to
Repetto for their toe shoes and tutus. Founded by the
mother of famed choreographer Roland Petit 50 years
ago, Repetto offers its own lines of everything for the
dancer, beginning with ballet slippers and the pink
Satin Opéra toe shoe (300F in sizes 6 to 24, medium
width) considered to be the most supple, lightweight,
and silent available.

If you have a dedicated ballerina at home with a
hard-to-fit foot, you may consider bringing an imprint
to the custom workshop for a tailor-made toe-shoe,
available in ten days. For the smallest ballerina, what
could be a greater inspiration than a hot pink four-
skirted tutu (285F in size 8)?

Besides the scores of dance shoe styles, there are
leotards, gymnastics attire, sweaters, and Repetto sig-
nature towels for the cooldown.

ADDRESS
40 Boulevard Haussemann, 9th
TELEPHONE
01.42.82.34.56
METRO
Chaussée d'Antin
OPEN
9:30AM to 6:30PM, Mon-Wed,
Fri-Sat; 9:30AM to 9PM, Thurs;
Sun in December
CREDIT CARDS
V, AE, MC
$$-$$$

42. GALERIES LAFAYETTE
Department store

Department store shopping in Paris has even less
ambiance than in the States, and is a vivid contrast to
the charm and service of Parisian boutiques. But it can
offer the hurried traveler an overview of the major
French labels and brands (helpful in deciding which
boutiques to visit after leaving), as well as one-stop
shopping, shipping, and a tax refund on the purchase
total.

When I have dreams about shopping, I'm always in
Galeries Lafayette. In no other Parisian department
store is the merchandise as upscale as here, where
100,000 customers a day come to search out
wardrobes, household goods, and gourmet foods.

Aimless wanderers can lose an entire day here. So
come when the doors open and you're feeling fresh. It
becomes so crowded by noon (all day on Saturdays)
that you'll have trouble moving through the throngs
and won't even notice the outstanding *belle époque* archi-
tecture.

If you plan to take advantage of the *détaxe* in addition to your 10 percent tourist discount, be sure to spend over 1,200F to qualify. Pick up a shopper's card (carnet) at the main-floor Visitor's Desk to carry with you, making sure the salesperson in each department uses it to record your purchases. When you're done shopping, take your form to the pick-up desk on the basement floor where you will pay for and collect your merchandise. Expect a wait of at least 20 minutes here. If you are not taking advantage of the discount, your salesperson will write up and package your purchases, but you must go to the department cashier to pay, then return with your receipt to pick up your packages.

The Galeries is really 110 departments in adjoining buildings. The store caters to Americans and you can get help in English at the welcome desk, as well as a 10 percent discount card available only to tourists. If it's fashion you're after, you may attend weekly runway shows (telephone 01.48.74.02.30 to reserve a seat), or even put yourself in the highly capable hands of *Mode Plus*, a complimentary in-store service that will outfit you in keeping with your budget and personal style. You're in the thick of French designers here, with a vast choice of both couture and *avant-garde* names on the first and second floors, many shown in their own mini-boutiques. If it's hot, you'll find it here, from the lower price ranges (their own stylish knockoff lines) to a main-floor Chanel boutique.

The main floor is a fertile hunting ground for presents (perfumes, leather goods, scarves, etc.). But don't miss children's wear, bed and table linens, housewares (you'll find Baccarat, etc., in the basement), and the very large gourmet food department with gold shopping carts and capped bellhops.

Menswear is in the neighboring Galfa Club building, and every *Maman* in Paris knows about the high-styled children's clothes (and more) in the moderately priced Monoprix next door.

Galeries Lafayette's rival department store, AU PRINTEMPS, is located across the street at 64 Boulevard Hausseman. Similar in service and offerings, the store has been redone in an American look.

Along the Way

The RUE DE RIVOLI is one of the most crowded, tourist-driven streets in Paris, but can hardly be avoided as it runs along the back side of the LOUVRE MUSEUM and TUILERIES GARDENS up to the PLACE DE LA CONCORDE. Its sheltering arcades can even be welcoming on a drizzly day, particularly if you're battling for a taxi. On a sunny day, don't miss the opportunity to detour through the gardens. Among the dozens of similar small shops announcing duty-free in their windows, you'll find a few worth a stop. For those interested in fashion (and who doesn't become so after a few days in Paris?), a visit to the MUSÉE DES ARTS DE LA MODE (the Louvre's costume museum at N.107 Rue de Rivoli) will put *haute couture* in perspective, and its 5th-floor gift boutique is a find for fans of retro fashion accessories. Next door is the MUSÉE DES ARTS DECORATIFS (N. 107 Rue de Rivoli), tracing the history of French homes from medieval times to the present through perfect period rooms, and a must for anyone who wants a background in French decorative style.

ADDRESS
248 Rue de Rivoli, 1st
TELEPHONE
01.44.77.88.99
METRO
Concorde
OPEN
9:30AM to 7PM, Mon-Sat;
1 to 6PM, Sun
CREDIT CARDS
V, AE, MC
$$

43. W. H. SMITH
Bookstore

All the best British, French, and English magazines are to be found here, along with thousands of books in English. This British-based store is one of the oldest in Paris to serve the English-reading public. The former tearoom space on the second floor now displays coffee-table books. There is a children's book section, a large travel section, and even a room for the French to read about travel in the United States and Britain.

44. DENISE FRANCELLE

Gloves for men and women and umbrellas

Mme Denise Francelle has been here since 1938, when this stretch of the arcades of the Rue de Rivoli housed many such gantiers (glovesellers). Among the competative tourist trade that lines the street today, this establishment does business as it always has, taking care to size properly and search out just the right glove from the tremendous inventory kept beneath the shop.

You'll find gloves for every occasion here, from classic to fantasy designs, from driving gloves to hand-pearled elbow gloves, even mink cuffs. Because Mme Francell has been buying for so long, you can find here many styles not available elsewhere, still at the original prices. And if it's not in her invertory, she will make to measure in any color. No wonder she has generations of repeat customers.

ADDRESS
244 Rue de Rivoli, 1st
TELEPHONE
01.42.60.76.15
METRO
Concorde
OPEN
10AM to 7PM, Mon-Sat
CREDIT CARDS
V, AE, MC
$$-$$$

45. MARECHAL

Limoges boxes and souvenirs

Go directly downstairs for the hand-painted Limoges porcelain boxes that are so varied and collectible, and so well-priced here. This 40-year-old establishment claims to have the largest selection in France, including copies of traditional designs as well as new ones, beginning at 300F. The Limoges factory produces the gamut of theme box shapes in white ceramic, and sells them to only a handful of artists authorized to decorate to Limoges' standard. Each is an individual work of art. On weekdays here, there is an artist authorized to personalize your piece.

Be sure to be added to the mailing list for the bi-annual brochure, which pictures a new group with the pricing in dollars, including U.S. delivery—a bargain compared to what you would pay back home. There is also a fine range of tourist trinkets that make thoughtful but inexpensive gifts; perhaps the Eiffel Tower keychain at 25F.

ADDRESS
232 Rue de Rivoli, 1st
TELEPHONE
01.42.60.71.83
FAX
01.42.60.33.76
METRO
Concorde
OPEN
10:30AM to 6:30PM, every day
CREDIT CARDS
V, AE, MC
$-$$$

 ANGELINA
Tea room

ADDRESS
226 Rue de Rivoli, 1st
TELEPHONE
01.42.60.82.00
METRO
Tuileries
OPEN
10AM to 6:30PM, daily; closed August
CREDIT CARDS
V, AE, MC

This tearoom is the beautiful big sister of Rumplemeyer's café in New York. Long-favored by children from the turn of the century, these now-grown grandes dames are seated amid the marble, murals, and mirrors, *en tête-à-tête* with friends or grandchildren. The place is equally popular with fashion models who retreat here after couture shows at the Louvre, and with shoppers wishing to escape the modern hordes. The famous hot chocolate is so rich that it shouldn't be consumed before noon.

ADDRESS
224 Rue de Rivoli, 1st
TELEPHONE
01.42.60.76.07
METRO
Tuileries
OPEN
10AM to 7PM, Mon-Sat
CREDIT CARDS
V, AE, MC
$$$

46. GALIGNANI
Bookstore

A classic bookstore, Galignani has been handed down from father to son since 1805. Though it is French, there is quite a selection of English and American books and an impressive collection of international art books. The beautiful interior naturally draws the book lover, and it is known as a very pleasant place to browse.

ADDRESS
206 Rue de Rivoli, 1st
TELEPHONE
01.42.60.51.17
FAX
01.93.20.74.51
METRO
Tuileries
OPEN
Oct 1 to May 30: 10AM to 7PM,
Mon-Sat; 11AM to 7PM, Sun
June 1 to Sept 30: 9:30AM to
7:30PM, Mon-Sat; 10:30AM to
7:30PM, Sun
CREDIT CARDS
V, AE, MC
$$

47. GAULT
Architectural miniatures

If you've always dreamed of a French period home made to old-world standards of craftsmanship, you'll find the practical answer here. The miniature ceramic homes and buildings entirely handmade by M. Gault's southern French workshops follow the architectural detailing of various regions of France. Each is carved from raw clay, sculpted, fired, and painted individually, and like the real thing, promises to last centuries. Moreover, they are portable and affordable (dream homes from 230 to 2,500F). You may want a tiny French bakery (45F) or to put together an entire Alsatian village, or your favorite neighborhood in

Paris. Gault also does specific buildings to order. Any
of these highly detailed recreations make terrific gifts.
Fax for the catalog to order from home.

The PLACE DU MARCHE ST-HONORE is a calm and fertile ground for creative
designer boutiques. Best-known are PHILIPPE MODEL (N.33) for his imaginative hats
(always a sensation at the Prix de Diane horse races, and unique at 1,500F for a custom
design) and funky to feminine shoes, belts, gloves, purses; and JEAN-CHARLES DE
CASTELBAJAC (N.31) for bold tongue-in-cheek fashions and home accessories.

 CAFÉ MARLY
Café and restaurant

ADDRESS
Cour Napoléon, 93 Rue de Rivoli, 1st
TELEPHONE
01.49.26.06.60
METRO
Palais-Royal
OPEN
8AM to 2AM, daily
CREDIT CARDS
V, AE, MC, DC

Located in the heart of Paris, overlooking the glass pyramid in the central courtyard of
the Louvre, Café Marly is a choice spot for a *rendez vous*. Even if you're not visiting the
museum, you will want to linger over a drink on the terrace as all of Paris walks by, or
take a light lunch in the sumptuous interior restaurant. Enter from the courtyard, Cour
Napoléon.

48. LE LOUVRE DES ANTIQUAIRES
Antiques

ADDRESS
2 Place du Palais-Royal, 1st
TELEPHONE
01.42.97.27.00
METRO
Palais-Royal
OPEN
11AM to 7PM, Tue-Sun
CREDIT CARDS
V, AE, MC
$$$-$$$$

Probably the world's most-shopped antiques center,
this cooperative of over 240 highly reputable dealers is
spread over three floors, providing civilized mall shop-
ping, complete with shipping agent and a good restau-
rant (Le Jardin du Louvre). Amid fine furniture and fur-
nishings from every century and continent you may
get carried away, but you won't get taken in, as these
dealers represent the most scrupulous and scrutinized
in the trade. Each piece is sold with a certificate of
guarantee, and the prices reflect it. On a rainy Sunday
you'll hardly find a better activity than to take a pro-
gram and wander the booths. Many of the dealers have
Left Bank shops with lower price tags. Pick up their
business cards if you're interested in their specialty.

Along the Way

Tranquil PALAIS-ROYAL was childhood home to Louis XIV, who nearly drowned in the garden fountains, as every French student learns. Today, you may see children playing hockey on roller skates in the palace courtyard. After centuries of ill-repute, the elegant quadrangle with the palace at one end, arcades along the three sides, and gardens in the center is experiencing a renaissance with shops at ground level and sought-after apartments above.

Colette wrote *Paris from My Window* from her own window overlooking the gardens. Former Minister of Culture Jack Lang (who is responsible for the controversial striped columns in the courtyard) has officed here, and resident Palais-Royalists feel they live at the most fortunate address in Paris.

La Boutique du Palais-Royal

ADDRESS
9 Rue de Beaujolais, 1st
TELEPHONE
01.42.60.08.22
METRO
Palais-Royal
OPEN
10AM to 7PM, Tue-Sat; 11AM to 7PM, Mon
CREDIT CARDS
V, AE
$$-$$$

49. LA BOUTIQUE DU PALAIS-ROYAL
Toys

Handcrafted toys, many of the sort meant to sit on your child's shelf forever, are here. The owner, Mme Baret, is influenced by the nearby Comédie Française (the French National Theater) to seek out those that add drama and originality to her shelves.

The marionettes by Jacques Picard in Provence are outstanding—especially the 2-foot-tall Puss in Boots with a painted face, knitted collars, and velour hat (990F). There is a complete selection of *santons* (rustic collector figurines from southern France), tiny tea sets, and doll furniture from the Louis-Philippe wooden armoires to cottage clay pieces acting as lounging ground for contented cats. Toy-happy adults will want to see the never-used pens from the '30s and '40s.

50. ANNA JOLIET
Music boxes

You might miss this tiny shop if not for the magical sounds floating out its door. Inside is a huge variety of music boxes for all ages and pocketbooks, with origins from Switzerland to Japan. From the simplest transparent square playing Mozart to elaborate antique instruments with new interior workings (1,500 to 2,500F), Anna Joliet offers them all, making this shop an attraction for the collector as well as a gift stop for the smallest child.

ADDRESS
9 Rue de Beaujolais, 1st
TELEPHONE
01.42.96.55.13
METRO
Palais-Royal
OPEN
10AM to 7PM, Tue-Sat; 2 to 7PM, Mon
CREDIT CARDS
V, MC
$-$$$

51. GALERIE CARMEN YNFANTE
Antique wedding dresses, romantic costumes, and accessories

As you approach the painted masks hanging on the window grills of her apartment upstairs from the gallery, you will know that Carmen Ynfante is a woman who lives her art. And she lives with it, surrounded by 2,000 wedding dresses in her living quarters (shown by appointment only), and more in the shop. The Spanish painter-sculptor-collector with flowing ashen tresses adorned by a crown of flowers and pearls (her own creation) sells these rich dresses from the '40s through the '60s for 1,500 to 2,500F; or she will rent them for 800F.

A peek into the shop is like a glimpse into a fairy godmother's attic, with hats (around 300F), purses, gloves, and jewelry dating from 1900 to 1960 and dresses of satin, embroideries, beading and hand-lace.

The personal service of Mme Ynfante and her assistant assure the bride of a proper fit, and the appropriate choice of headwear.

ADDRESS
44 & 45 Galerie de Montpensier, 1st
TELEPHONE
01.47.03.35.99 (boutique); 42.61.46.98 (studio)
METRO
Palais-Royal
OPEN
1:30 to 7:30PM, Mon-Sat or by appointment
NO CREDIT CARDS
$-$$

Galerie Carmen Ynfante

Galerie Carmen Ynfante

ADDRESS
34 Galerie Montpensier, 1st
TELEPHONE
01.40.20.00.11
METRO
Palais-Royal
OPEN
10AM to 7PM, Mon-Sat; Sun
afternoons
CREDIT CARDS
AE
$$

52. LES DRAPEAUX DE FRANCE
Lead soldiers

Little boys press their noses to these windows to get a better view of the armies of thousands of soldiers on display in this phone-booth-size shop. Foot soldiers from most any Western war are 140F, with cavaliers at 250F. Next door they can purchase military decorations from around the world.

ADDRESS
19-20 Galerie Montpensier, 1st
(Couture)
23-24 Galerie Montpensier, 1st
(Accessories)
TELEPHONE AND FAX
01.42.96.06.56
METRO
Palais-Royal
OPEN
11AM to 7PM, Mon-Sat; 1 to
7PM, Sun
CREDIT CARDS
V, AE
$$-$$$

53. DIDIER LUDOT
Vintage couture clothing, shoes, leather goods

This is where Parisians come to find their original Hermès "Kelly" bags, reworked crocodile luggage, stiletto heels that really are from the '50s, and their postwar-era Chanel suits. Didier Ludot is the city's prime vendor of couture clothing and leather goods from the '30s through the '70s, and the racks are filled with labels like Dior, Grès, Balmain, and Jacques Fath at prices beginning under 1,000F.

If you've never done secondhand shopping, keep in mind that the evening gowns and daywear that may look a bit worn carry a great mystique and simply cannot be had new. The handbags and luggage, also bearing grand labels and often from exotic materials, are reconditioned to endure well into the next century.

ADDRESS
172 Galerie de Valois, 1st
TELEPHONE
01.42.96.04.24
FAX
01.42.61.46.54
METRO
Palais-Royal
OPEN
1:30 to 7PM, Mon-Sat
CREDIT CARDS
V
$$$-$$$$

54. MANUFACTURE DU PALAIS ROYAL
Tableware, new and antique

Craftsman Dominique Paramythiotis has restored the word *manufacture* to its orginal meaning: "made by hand." Known for his high standards in carrying on the tradition of handmade fine china delicately painted with 18 karat gold, he has created personal designs for such clients as Yves St. Laurent.

Each piece carrying the Manufacture du Palais-Royal name is conceptualized and produced by the master himself, and displayed in the shop alongside porcelains and earthenware from the 17th through 19th centuries. Over 100 patterns are offered in this sumptuous collection (dinner plates begin at 500F),

with accessory pieces ranging from candlesticks to ash-
trays.

A must for lovers of fine china, this is the place to
come for your formal service, or to pick up a beautiful
object for your table.

Along the Way

Continue on the GALERIE DE VALOIS for more notable boutiques devoted to the
home: LA VIE DE CHATEAU (N.157 Galerie de Valois and N.17 Rue de Valois) is a
superb shop specializing in 18th- through 20th-century table arts such as one might find
in the cupboards of a chateau; MURIEL GRATEAU (N.132 & N.133 Galerie de Valois)
shows the designer's own line of contemporary tableware and fashion mixed with her
antique collections.

☕ RESTAURANT DU PALAIS ROYAL

Address
110 Galérie de Valois
TELEPHONE
01.40.20.00.27
METRO
Palais-Royal
OPEN
Mid-morning until 2AM

On most days, tables are set up in the Palais-Royal gardens, where you can spend a
happy hour with a flute of champagne or over an open-air meal that can go courses
beyond a typical picnic. This is a lovely spot to enjoy some sun and a cup of coffee. In
wet weather everything moves indoors to a modern setting.

If you're in the mood for something more historical, head toward LE GRAND VEFOUR
(N.17 Rue de Beaujolais) one of the city's most charming restaurants, where famous
names have feasted and conversed since the days when Napoleon dined here with
Josephine. (Luncheon menu at 325F; dinners about 750F.)

Before leaving Palais-Royal you might stop into BEL GAZOU (N.5, Rue des Petits-
Champs), an old-fashioned magazine shop, to pick up photo-reproduction post cards of
an older Paris (5F) and writing pens. The owners promise to procure for you any book
in Paris within 48 hours of your order.

☕ WILLI'S WINE BAR

ADDRESS
13 Rue des Petits-Champs, 1st
TELEPHONE
01.42.61.05.09
METRO
Palais-Royal or Bourse
OPEN
Noon to 2:30PM & 7 to 11PM, Mon-Sat
CREDIT CARDS
V, MC

When the wine is as important as the company, a rendezvous over a carafe at the corner cafe just won't do. The Parisian who wants to pick and choose his vintage from small production wines to familiar favorites will go to a wine bar to taste and test. There he can order by the bottle or glass from quality house selections, often hand-picked by the bar owner at the vinyard and shipped in barrels directly to the bar.

At Willi's, among the most popular and elegant of these *bars à vins*, Englishman Mark Williamson will help you choose from 300 labels the bottle that is perfectly attuned to your entree or salad.

The nearby GALERIE VIVIENNE is a smartly renovated glass-vaulted shopping arcade, where the traditional proprietors are almost outnumbered by fashionable new boutiques. At YUKI TORII (N.38-40 Galerie Vivienne) you'll be able to find something original, colorful, and clever to add to your wardrobe; around the corner at PYLONES a rubber bow tie is a must. Under the arched glass skylight at A PRIORI THE (N.35-37 Galerie Vivienne) is a charming spot to sit with tea and brownie, a light lunch, or weekend brunch.

Among the Galerie Vivienne's original tenants was DOMINIQUE ET FRANÇOIS JOUSSEAUME (N.45-47 Galerie Vivienne), a warmly wooded book and prints shop with merchandise that has been obtained anytime since 1826 and LEGRAND FILLE ET FILS (N.12 Galerie Vivienne, but for the full effect of its 19th-century storefront go around to N. 1 Rue de la Banque), where the all-time bestseller is a little gingerbread pig sold as a good-luck charm among bins of hard candy and shelves of wine bottles and preserves.

55. JEAN-PAUL GAULTIER
Women's and men's clothing

Certainly the most provocative Paris designer, perhaps the most outrageous, the Gaultier look is favored by Madonna, and both personify a modern version of the baroque esthetic.

Whether or not you would be comfortable in Gaultier, his past collections have pointed toward the future of fashion and a peek into his boutique promises to be a trip to another planet or a brilliant vision of the future, depending on your sensibilities; either way it's fun and well worth it. You'll be surrounded by videos of his latest collection (they're even set into the Pompeiian tile floor), and metal manequins, reminding you that Gaultier is out to create the future on the ruins of our past. He's a designer who knows his history, being classically trained by Cardin and Patou, and has even received the coveted French Fashion Oscar.

The flagship store on St-Antoine also houses his furniture collection, and here you can sometimes find a limited edition item of clothing from the design studios upstairs.

ADDRESS
6 Rue Vivienne, 2nd (enter from the street)
TELEPHONE
01.42.86.05.05
METRO
Bourse

ADDRESS
30 Rue St-Antoine, 11th
PHONE
01.44.68.85.00
METRO
Bastille
OPEN
10AM to 7PM, Mon-Fri; 11AM to 7PM, Sat
CREDIT CARDS
V, AE, MC, DC
$$$-$$$$

56. MOHOLY-NAGY
Men's and women's shirts and blouses

For stylishly simple variations on the white shirt, this is your stop. The classic backdrops that French women collect in numbers are harder to locate in the States. For men the variety comes in colors. Functionalism runs in the family of American-raised André Moholy-Nagy, grandson of the founder of the American School of Design in Chicago. Interesting little details may go nearly unnoticed on these clean cuts in cotton, silk, viyella, and lace, but the overall effect is smashing. Prices begin at about 600F.

ADDRESS
2 Galerie Vivienne, 2nd
TELEPHONE
01.40.15.05.33
METRO
Bourse
OPEN
10AM to 2:30PM and 3 to 7PM, Mon-Fri; noon to 7PM, Sat
CREDIT CARDS
V
$$-$$$

ADDRESS
34 Galerie Vivienne, 2nd
TELEPHONE
01.42.60.46.85
METRO
Bourse
OPEN
9:30AM to7PM, Mon-Fri;
10:30AM to1PM & 1:30 to
6:30PM, Sat

ADDRESS
27 Boulevard Raspail, 6th
TELEPHONE
01.45.48.30.97
METRO
Rue du Bac
OPEN
10AM to 1PM & 2 to 6:45PM,
Tue-Sat

ADDRESS
58 Avenue Paul-Doumer, 16th
TELEPHONE
01.45.03.42.75
METRO
Muette
OPEN
10AM to7PM, Mon-Sat
CREDIT CARDS
V, AE
$$

57. CASA LOPEZ
Needlepoint

You will recognize the ravishing Casa Lopez petit point pillows at finely decorated addresses all around town now that Véronique Lopez has brought them back into style. Her romantic raised designs of bows, florals, traditional Victorian and Greek patterns, and geometrics are woven by hand (except for certain carpeting) in her Portuguese workshop supplied with 90 shades of threads. The technique is ancient, dating from the Renaissance when the threads were embroidered onto fishnets, but the look is fresh and just the thing to recover those old Louis XIV dining chairs, or to make a splash on the floor.

Carpets are sold by the meter, and can be customized to decorating perfection from 5,000F per square meter, with cute little rugs beginning at 900F. You can purchase a cushion cover (600-900F), or needle point an identical one at home with a Casa Lopez kit.

Along the Way

The PLACE DES VICTOIRES is prime real estate for fashion-forward boutiques whose designs have been termed avant-garde anytime from the recent past to the near future. Many of these designers are established, but certainly not passé. It's also a hunting ground for wardrobe shoppers eager for a bird's-eye view of the coming season.

58. KENZO
Women's, men's, junior, children's clothing

East and West have come to meet in the designs of Kenzo, the most successful and the most French of Japanese designers in Paris. A tourist who stayed on after top honors from his fashion school back home, Kenzo introduced wild mixes of colors, patterns, and aspects of Japanese tailoring that have permanently broadened French fashion.

Enormously successful in the East and West, Kenzo reflects both cultures in a look that's fresh and fun to wear. The Place des Victoires boutique carries his women's line *(Paris)*, some of the junior lines (not so wild as they once seemed), and some men's. The appealing Kenzo look is abundant here, and pricing is at its best during the January and July 50 percent off sales.

ADDRESS
3 Place des Victoires, 1st
(Women's, men's)
TELEPHONE
01.40.39.72.03
METRO
Bourse

ADDRESS
16 Boulevard Raspail, 6th
(Women's, children's)
TELEPHONE
01.42.22.09.38
METRO
Bac

ADDRESS
17 Boulevard Raspail, 6th
(Men's)
TELEPHONE
01.45.49.33.75
METRO
Bac

ADDRESS
18 Avenue Georges V, 8th
(Women's, men's)
TELEPHONE
01.47.23.33.49
METRO
Alma-Marçeau

ADDRESS
60-62 Rue de Rennes, 6th
(Juniors')
TELEPHONE
01.45.44.27.88
METRO
St-Sulpice

ADDRESS
99 Rue de Passy, 16th (Juniors', men's)
TELEPHONE
01.42.24.92.92
METRO
Passy
OPEN
10AM to 7PM, Mon; 10AM to 7PM, Tue-Sat
CREDIT CARDS
V, AE, DC
$$$

ADDRESS
6 Place des Victoires, 2nd
TELEPHONE
01.42.61.60.74
METRO
Bourse

ADDRESS
13 Bis Rue de Grenelle, 7th
TELEPHONE
01.42.22.93.03
METRO
St-Sulpice
OPEN
10:30AM to 7PM, Mon-Sat

ADDRESS
36 Rue Sévigny, 3rd
TELEPHONE
01.42.77.87.91
METRO
St-Paul
OPEN
10:30AM to 12:15PM & 1:15 to
7PM, Mon-Sat; 2 to 7PM, Sun

ADDRESS
20 Avenue Victor-Hugo, 16th
TELEPHONE
01.45.00.44.41
METRO
Victor-Hugo
CREDIT CARDS
V, AE
$$$

59. STÉPHEN KELIAN
Men's and women's shoes

Stéphen Kelian's trademark is a woven shoe that doesn't squeak, but whispers. The clientele attuned to his brand of high-fashion sobriety can well understand his high prices. Not just plain brown loafers, these wovens have the versatile palette of an Oriental carpet, and the shapes to carry off your new wardrobe from *Victoire*. You'll find well-heeled models that are unavailable outside France, particularly at the trendy Rue de Grenelle boutique. The men's line includes his designs for Jean-Paul Gaultier.

ADDRESS
10-12 Place des Victoires, 2nd
TELEPHONE
01.42.60.96.21 or 42.61.09.02
METRO
Bourse

ADDRESS
16 Rue de Passy, 16th
TELEPHONE
01.42.88.20.84
METRO
Passy
OPEN
10AM to 7PM, Mon-Sat
CREDIT CARDS
V, AE
$$$

60. VICTOIRE
Women's clothes

If you've come to Paris for clothes, make Victoire an early stop. Known for the quick and clever way it puts together the newest European designer looks, you can't do better than by asking the staff here to pull something together for you, complete with bag, belt, and scarf.

At the original Place des Victoires location, the boutique at N.10 showcases younger, less established, more affordable lines, while those next door at N.12 are the big names. The collections arrive here earlier than most stores: mid-August for fall-winter and December for spring-summer.

Along the Way

Fashion trekkies should continue down the RUE ETIENNE-MARCEL. Don't miss BARBARA BUI's poetic designs in flowing silks next to her crisply cut leathers (N.23); CHEVIGNON TRADING POST (N.49), as much a movie set of the Old West as a store full of everything the French would want to outfit their homesteads, from Pendleton blankets to the popular Chevignon leather jackets; EN ATTENDANT DES BARBARES (N.50), house of hip home decor, much of it portable.

61. EQUIPMENT
Women's and men's shirts

French friends tell me they all come here for their silk shirts and silk T-shirts, both indispensable to *Parisiennes* of all ages. It's no wonder when you see your favorite classic shirt on the rack in 25 colors (from 900F), and the perfect summer T-shirt in 14 colors. Telling details like a French cuff, dressy button, or a discreet pleat can dress up or down. Equipment now offers cottons for summer and plaids, polka dots, and abstracts for variety. The newest look here is a narrow-cut silk jersey.

ADDRESS
46 Rue Etienne-Marcel, 2nd
TELEPHONE
01.40.26.17.84
METRO
Etienne-Marcel

ADDRESS
203 Boulevard St-Germain, 6th
TELEPHONE
01.45.48.86.82
METRO
Rue du Bac
OPEN
10:30AM to 7:30PM, Mon-Sat
CREDIT CARDS
V, AE
$$$

ADDRESS
36 Rue Etienne-Marcel, 2nd;
48 Rue Montmartre, 2nd
TELEPHONE
01.42.33.71.65
METRO
Etienne-Marcel
OPEN
8:30AM to 6PM, Mon-Sat
CREDIT CARDS
V, MC
$$

62. A. SIMON
Kitchen accessories

The light and calm atmosphere that prevails here, and the very helpful sales staff make this an easy stop for cooks. Come to the main shop (Rue Etienne-Marcel) for the lovely white porcelain dishes (plates from 15F), salt and pepper sets (92F), decanters, mustard jars, and so forth, that are typically found in French cafés.

Simply cross the street (through the courtyard at 48 Rue Montmartre) for professional cookwear, knives, cheese servers, and pastry molds. The establishment is happy to ship.

ADDRESS
18-20 Rue Coquillière, 1st
TELEPHONE
01.42.36.53.13
FAX
01.45.08.86.83
METRO
Les Halles
OPEN
8AM to 12:30PM & 2 to 6PM,
Mon; 8AM to 6PM Tue-Sat
CREDIT CARDS
V, MC
$-$$$

63. DEHILLERIN
Kitchen utensils

A trip to this remarkable establishment, where the Dehillerin family has been in residence since 1820, is an unforgettable experience. Even if you think you already have every knickknack necessary for a well-equipped kitchen, a look around Dehillerin will show you the many ways you could stock your *batterie de cuisine*.

Shelves, floor, and ceiling are stocked with an exhaustively impressive supply of kitchenware from copper pots (properly lined with nickel at 990F for a set of five) large enough to feed all the king's men, to tiny chocolate molds of infinite variety.

Restaurant chefs bump shoulders with housewives in an effort to locate just the right tool. Professional-size cookware is in the basement.

Though the store will ship, I never leave here without something in hand, be it a basic omelette pan to inspire small cooks at home or a pretty pastry shaper for a friend. Ask for the English catalog, covering a selection of knives, serving pieces, molds, and copper cookware so you can show the sales staff exactly what you want. Or fax for it from the States and send back a list of items that interest you, requesting prices and a shipping estimate. You may pay by mail with credit card or bank draft.

64. AGNÈS B.
Men's, women's and children's clothing

Agnès B. has won over Parisians with her deceptively simple styling and affordable price tags. Color and cut are outstanding and the look is casual, comfortable, and chic. Fabrics are natural and prices reasonable.

From her domaine of four boutiques on the Rue de Jour, this knowing mother of five has brought her understated sophistication to entire families. A harried American mother can let her husband and children loose on the street, retreat into the shop at N.6, allowing the salesgirl to outfit her from head to toe (shoes and makeup are upstairs), and emerge alluringly French. Agnès understands how to bring the same discreet allure to a working woman or preteen "Lolita."

If these quiet clothes don't speak to you from the rack, slip on a colored cotton cardigan with pearl snaps (400F at N.6, less at LOLITA) and you'll understand what they're saying.

ADDRESS
6 Rue du Jour, 1st (Women's)
TELEPHONE
01.45.08.56.56

ADDRESS
2 Rue du Jour, 1st (Children to 12 years and maternity)
TELEPHONE
01.40.39.96.88

ADDRESS
3 Rue du Jour, 1st (Men's)
TELEPHONE
01.42.33.34.13
METRO
Les Halles

ADDRESS
10 Rue du Jour, 1st (Lolita, junior girls)
TELEPHONE
01.45.08.49.89
METRO
Les Halles

ADDRESS
22 Rue St-Sulpice, 6th (Men's)
TELEPHONE
01.40.51.70.69
METRO
St-Sulpice

ADDRESS
13 Rue Michelet, 6th (Women's)
TELEPHONE
01.46.33.70.20
METRO
Luxembourg

ADDRESS
17 Avenue Pierre I de Serbie, 16th (Men's and women's)
TELEPHONE
01.47.20.27.35
METRO
Alma-Marçeau or Iéna
OPEN
Noon to 7PM, Mon; 10:30AM to 7PM, Tue-Sat
CREDIT CARDS
V, AE
$$-$$$

ADDRESS
8 Rue du Jour, 1st
TELEPHONE
01.40.26.76.70
METRO
Les Halles
OPEN
10AM to 7PM, Mon-Fri;
10:30AM to 7PM, Sat
CREDIT CARDS
V, AE
$$$-$$$$

65. CLAUDE VELL
Children's clothing

Children will run through the flower-filled courtyard off the Rue du Jour to the two tiled cottages that are Claude Vell's. This little-publicized designer makes clothes that stand out because they are so comfortable and subdued. Mostly in calm solids or stripes, never branded with a logo, every item is of a natural fabric and easy to wear. There are wide-wale cords with jackets, and sweatshirt dresses for little ones, all beautifully made. Next door are more grown-up, dressed-down designs to age 16.

Claude Vell

66. LA DROGUERIE
Dressmaker's trimmings

On Saturdays crowds line up at this bright and well-lit shop to find just the right touch for the outfits of their fantasies. Colorful yarns in cotton, wool, alpaca, tinsel, and chenille are sold by the 100 grams (3.5 oz. at 40 to 64F) along with very original knitting patterns. Embroidered ribbons from around Europe evoke the past or modernity in vinyl. There are buttons, beads, and jewelry-making items stocked in hundreds of little wooden drawers behind the sales counter. Fruits, flowers, and feathers are inviting adornments for the plain straw and felt hats.

Even if you enter feeling uninspired, there are plenty of imaginative examples of what you might knit, needlepoint, or string together on display. If you have an idea in mind, the salesladies will help you in your quest.

ADDRESS
9 & 11 Rue du Jour, 1st
TELEPHONE
01.45.08.93.27
METRO
Les Halles
OPEN
2 to 6:45PM, Mon; 10:30AM to 6:45PM, Tue-Sat
NO CREDIT CARDS
$

67. CLAUDIE PIERLOT
Women's clothes

Another member of the fashion school of discretion, Claudie Pierlot offers a preppy look with charm. A few basic colors and sporty shapes make up the collection, which gives itself to easy mix-and-matching. You can find some dressier items here than at Agnès B., and prices are somewhat lower.

ADDRESS
1 Rue Montmartre, 1st
TELEPHONE
01.42.21.38.38
METRO
Les Halles

ADDRESS
23 Rue du Vieux-Colombier, 6th
TELEPHONE
01.45.48.11.96
METRO
St-Sulpice
OPEN
1 to 7PM, Mon; 10:30AM to 7PM, Tue-Sat
CREDIT CARDS
V, AE
$$-$$$

ADDRESS
5 Rue Montmartre, 2nd
TELEPHONE
01.40.41.99.51
METRO
Les Halles

ADDRESS
23 Rue de Grenelle, 7th
TELEPHONE
01.45.49.28.73
METRO
Rue du Bac
OPEN
2 to 7PM, Mon; 10:30 to
12:30AM & 1 to 7PM, Tue-Sat
CREDIT CARDS
V AE MC
$$

ADDRESS
14 Rue Turbigo, 1st
TELEPHONE
01.42.33.44.36
METRO
Les Halles
OPEN
9:30AM to 6:30PM, Mon-Sat
NO CREDIT CARDS
$$

68. PRINCESSE TAM TAM
Lingerie

If you're planning a day in the country, in your under-wear, come to Princesse Tam Tam to buy it. Mostly cottons, with nothing transparent or peekaboo, the cut remains feminine, even without much lace. Denim stitching or floral prints in dark colors are the look here. It's perfect for teens, and for women of the world who love to feel cozy in their jams.

69. DUTHILLEUL & MINART
Professional uniforms

If you're giving a formal dinner and the caterer doesn't show, you'll be able to dress the part after a trip to Duthilleul & Minart, a shop with everything from the chef's *toque* (hat) and waiter's *tablier* (apron) to the *bleus de travail* (blue cotton work clothes) that are worn by more French than any couture label.

This place is all business, and while the dressing rooms are not elegant, a tailor is on staff to assure that even the corner butcher leaves with a perfect fit. There are also traditional craftsmen's uniforms and a large selection of restaurant-quality dish towels.

70. LE CÈDRE ROUGE

Outdoor furniture and garden accessories

The garden pieces overflowing into the Place Victoria are an invitation to enter this gardener's Eden. As you do, be sure to pick up a house card at the main desk for jotting down notes as you explore the diverse collection of handsome patio furniture that includes striking wrought-iron tables with green-glazed ceramic tops, 18th-century reproductions, and postmodern chaises. In the second entrance are flowerpots and urns coming from regional France and Italy, rustic basketry, citronella candles (45F) to ward off garden bugs, and an irresistible supply of small hostess gifts.

Though much of what you'll see won't fit into your suitcase, the store will handle shipping when pressed.

ADDRESS
22 Avenue Victoria, 1st
TELEPHONE
01.42.33.71.05
METRO
Châtelet
OPEN
10AM to 6:30PM, Tue-Sat
CREDIT CARDS
V, AE
$$-$$$

Le Cèdre Rouge

71. LE JARDIN DE VICTORIA

Garden tools, seeds, plants

After Le Cèdre Rouge, come next door to buy authentically French seeds for your victory garden. This gardener's supply house has been on the Place Victoria since 1925, selling its own packaged seeds, plants, and practical garden tools.

You may want to bring home *sachets* (seed packets) of *haricots fins* (French green beans), herbs, endive, or choose from among 15 different types of lettuce or hundreds of flower seeds. At 10F for most packets, a tiny investment can nurture a high-grossing yield.

You may want to fax ahead for their catalog.

ADDRESS
24 Avenue Victoria, 1st
TELEPHONE
01.42.33.84.07
FAX
01.45.08.89.80
METRO
Châtelet
OPEN
9:30AM to 6PM, Tue-Sat
NO CREDIT CARDS
$

The Marais

The maze of cobblestone streets that form the
MARAIS (named for the "marsh" it was before it was
drained and became the fashionable center of Paris in
the 1400s) naturally deter traffic, but lure the adven-
turesome shopper who doesn't care to see crowds of
fellow tourists. It's the French who flock here on weekends, anxious to explore a neighborhood where artisans live and trade next door to film stars, and fashionable boutiques thrive behind ancient facades.

A declared historic district of primarily medieval
and renaissance buildings, the Marais is wedged
between those modern architectural statements, the
BEAUBOURG and the BASTILLE OPERA, but has
ably avoided the gentrification that often follows the
crowds. This is a neighborhood in which to *flâner*, or
wander and browse as the French do.

The serious tourist may want to stop first at the
CENTRE CULTUREL DU MARAIS, 28 Rue des
Francs-Bourgeois, for a detailed map of the area and
information on the music and arts festival that takes
place here in June and July.

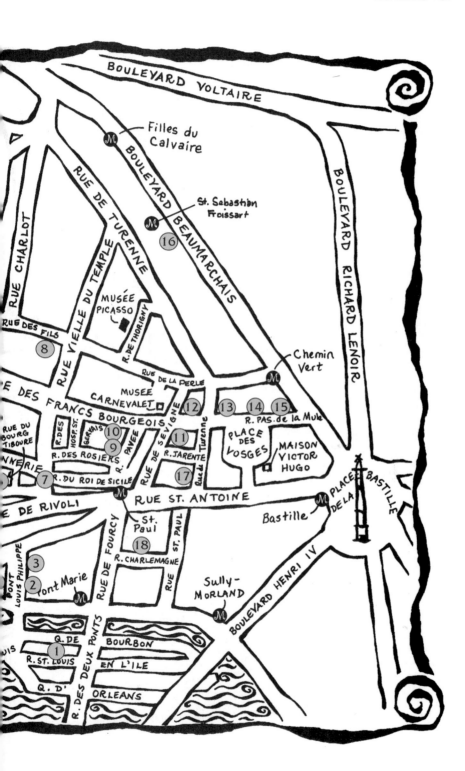

Where to Stay

HOTEL DU JEU DE PAUME

ADDRESS
54 Rue Saint-Louis-en-Ile, 4th
TELEPHONE
01.43.26.14.18
FAX
01.40.46.02.76
METRO
Pont-Marie
Double rooms from 900F;
Breakfast 80F
CREDIT CARDS
V, AE, MC

The deluxe hotel on the island has a wood and stone interior, a glass elevator, and every pampering amenity. Ask for a room over the courtyard.

HOTEL DE LA BRETONNERIE

ADDRESS
22 Rue Saint-Croix-de-la-
Bretonnerie, 4th
TELEPHONE
01.48.87.77.63
FAX
01.42.77.26.78
METRO
Hôtel-de-Ville
Double rooms from 650F;
Breakfast 45F
CREDIT CARDS
V, MC

Set in a 17th-century townhouse on a quiet street, you can almost forget you're in the thick of an area that's lively night and day. This popular hotel has marble bathrooms and Louis XII decor.

HOTEL DES DEUX-ILES

ADDRESS
59 Rue St-Louis-en-Ile, 4th
TELEPHONE
01.43.26.13.35
FAX
01.43.29.60.25
METRO
Pont-Marie
Doubles from 680F;
Breakfast 45F
NO CREDIT CARDS

Cosy and charming, this tiny hotel has rooms decorated in pretty Provençal prints with great views from the top, a lounging lobby below, and the allure of the island outside its doors.

Culture Along the Way

MUSEE CARNAVALET

The graceful 17th-century townhouse and gardens that were home to the Marquise de Sévigné (who documented her own times in her famed letters) now house the venerable history of Paris in furniture, documents, and objects including even the letter Robespierre was writing when the Revolutionaries found him in his tub. Open 10AM to 5:40PM, Tue-Sun; closed Mon.

ADDRESS
23 Rue de Sévigné, 3rd
METRO
Saint-Paul

MUSEE PICASSO

Picasso's favorite pieces were passed on to his heirs, whose donations to the state in lieu of inheritance taxes are now the world's definitive Picasso collection, on view in a 16th-century mansion. Open 9:30AM to 5:30PM, Mon & Wed-Sun; closed Tue.

ADDRESS
5 Rue Thorigney, 3rd
METRO
Saint-Paul

MAISON VICTOR HUGO

In a former private home where the writer lived from 1832 to 1948 are souvenirs and drawings left by the writer, and a great view of the Place des Vosges from his top window. Open: 10AM to 5:40PM, Tue-Sun; closed Mon.

ADDRESS
6 Place des Vosges, 4th
METRO
Saint-Paul or Bastille

Marais Shops

ADDRESS
9 Quai de Bourbon, 4th
TELEPHONE
01.46.33.21.27
METRO
Pont-Marie
OPEN
12:30 to 7:30PM, Tue-Sat
CREDIT CARDS
V
$$$

1. MERI DIEM
Bed linens and sleepwear

These superb linens are modern classics, and in the tra-
ditional manner, Claire Dumail works to custom order
in the loft above her light-wooded shop where samples
in shades of white, ecru, and honey-colored cottons
and linens hang from simple black rods. Ask to feel the
métis, a cotton-linen fabric with a wonderful hand (and
lower-priced than pure linen) that you won't find back
home. Hand-smocking, cording and monograms are
beautifully executed on bed linens whose ornamenta-
tion extends only to the most understated buttons,
bows, and flanges. An assortment of companion
kimonos and nightshirts are available off the rack.
American bed sizes are no problem (see sizing chart),
and within 4-6 weeks your linens can be picked up at
the *atelier* or shipped. Prices are in keeping with quality:
a sheet with two pillowcases runs 1500 to 3500F; a
comforter cover with 2 cases is 2,300 to 4,000F.

Meri Diem

2. CALLIGRANE
Stationary and Desk Accessories

For those who shift into *mode moderne* at work,
Calligrane will have the necessary *funtionabilia* to dress
your desk. Under ornately tiled ceilings are calculators
to briefcases, staplers to agendas, in top Euro-designs
that will captivate the contemporary critic. Black, red,
and chrome reign in accessories, while the papers next
door offer the rainbow.

Select a string-stitched sketch book from Austria
with handmade papers and a red skin to capture Paris
by pen (390F), or letter paper that cleverly folds into
an envelope. An unusual selection of paper sizes,
shapes, colors, and materials lends itself to the particular client, and engraving is offered. Both stores are
good gift stops, especially for an inscrutable male.

ADDRESS
4 Rue du Pont-Louis-Philippe,
4th (Desk accessories)
TELEPHONE
01.48.04.31.89

ADDRESS
6 Rue du Pont-Louis-Philipe,
4th (Stationery)
TELEPHONE
01.40.27.00.74
FAX
01.40.27.84.08
METRO
Saint-Paul
OPEN
11AM to 7PM, Tue-Sat
CREDIT CARDS
V
$$-$$$

Calligrane

3. MELODIES GRAPHIQUES
Stationery and desk accessories

ADDRESS
10 Rue du Pont-Louis-Philippe, 4th
TELEPHONE
01.42.74.57.88
METRO
Saint-Paul
OPEN
11AM to 7PM, Tue-Sat
CREDIT CARDS
V, AE, MC
$$$

The fine Florentine papers found here are not for the modernist. These marbelized finishes are for the romantic writer and most every paper, pencil and notebook is finished with a bath of dyes whose endless variations have fascinated since the process was created by the bookbinder to the court of Louis XIII.

Journals and stationery in vivid butterfly colorations lend themselves to literary prose, and the agendas (120F) and desk organizers are just the touch for a home library. A selection of lovely marbelized boxes in the shapes of hearts (60F), butterflies, and crescent moons is easy to pack and carry home to delighted friends.

4. PAPIER PLUS
Stationery products

ADDRESS
9 Rue du Pont Louis Philippe, 4th
TELEPHONE
01.42.77.70.49
METRO
Saint-Paul
OPEN
Noon to 7PM, Mon-Sat
CREDIT CARDS
V
$$

Architects, artists, and fastidious laymen drop in from around the world to stock up on this exclusive supply of canvas-covered journals and portfolios meticulously executed by designer Laurent Tisné.

Formerly a publisher of art books, Tisné has brought his high standards and a strong graphic sense to the Papier Plus line. The formula for his popular "little white book" has expanded to 8 formats and 14 solid colors in various dimensions and paper qualities from 80-140F, each volume beautiful and book-like enough to say "Keep me."

Come here for photo albums, address books, stationery and more, neatly arranged by color on simple wooden shelves. The second entrance holds drawing papers and larger portfolios.

Papier Plus

5. BAZAR DE L'HOTEL DE VILLE (BHV)

Department store for home improvements

While it's not very *touristique*, the basement of the BHV is one of the most frequented retail spaces in Paris. A mecca of hardware and home improvement supplies, in styles designed to fit into the most historic or modern of domiciles, makes the trip down the central staircase a cultural experience.

Go to aisle N.7 for latches and doorknobs in keeping with your Louis XVI furnishings or your contemporary castle, or for something hand-forged. You'll find beautiful bronze dinner bells (from 43F), voluptuous bathroom fixtures as well as old-fashioned and newfangled tools for the handyman in this basement bazaar. On the fourth floor is an equally broad variety of moderately priced upholstery fabrics, custom wood paneling, and window coverings such as the white lace and embroidered shades so hard to come by in the States. For fun, pick up the 100-page order guide. Purchases over 1,500F will be delivered free of charge, in town.

Just outside the store on the Rue de Rivoli is a stand that sells common French signs. You might euphemise your guest bath with a plaque identifying the correct *"toilette,"* or provide a gentle reminder to your household to keep the door shut with the gift of a *"fermez"* sign to hang over the knob.

ADDRESS
52-56 Rue de Rivoli, 4th
TELEPHONE
01.42.74.90.00
METRO
Hôtel-de-Ville
OPEN
9:30AM to 7PM, Mon-Tue & Thurs-Sat; 9:30AM to 10PM, Wed
CREDIT CARDS
V, AE
$-$$

 MARIAGE FRÈRES
Tea salon and shop

ADDRESS
30-32 Rue du Bourg-Tibourg, 4th
TELEPHONE
01.42.72.28.11
METRO
Hôtel de Ville
ADDRESS
13 Rue des Grands-Augustins, 6th
METRO
St-Michel
TELEPHONE
01.40.51.82.5
OPEN
Noon to 7:30PM, Tue-Sun (Tea Salon)
10AM to 7:30PM, daily (Boutique)
CREDIT CARDS
V, AE, MC

Mariage Frères has been France's leading tea importer since 1854, and in this salon-boutique has made a beautiful marriage of Eastern and Western traditions centered around the drinking of tea. In an exotic rattan- and palm-furnished salon you can sip your choice of over 400 teas to the strains of European arias.

Behind the scenes, master tea-makers still cut and stitch your tea bag by hand, while the dark counters up front are laden with varieties of loose teas (from 12 to 45F per 100 grams), teapots either antique or authentically copied, and lovely tea services. A brunch that may be juice, eggs and salmon, pastry, tea, and toasts is served from noon to 6 (120F); lunch is served noon to 3PM, and a formal tea takes place from 3 to 7PM. This is a must for tea lovers, but others take warning—coffee is not available!

ADDRESS
7 Rue de Moussy, 4th
ADDRESS
18 Rue de la Verrierie, 4th
(outlet)
TELEPHONE
01.42.72.19.19
METRO
Hôtel de Ville
OPEN
10AM to 7PM, Mon-Sat
CREDIT CARDS
V, AE, DC
$$$$

6. AZZEDINE ALAIA
Women's clothes

This tiny Tunisian is in the forefront of creators with wild and slinky clothes that would change a doormouse into a femme fatale. Alaia's magic sissors are reputed to sculpt the body to the curves of the garment, a wile that fashion writers and artistic celebrities from Paloma Picasso to Tina Turner can't seem to deny themselves.

No less wild is the loft-like boutique designed with New York artist Julien Schnabel, where each sparce piece of furniture has a personality and forged-iron sculptures double as clothes racks. Buzz the building for admittance. Just around the corner, in a tamer space, is last season's collection at 30 to 50 percent off.

7. STOCK GRIFFES
Discount women's clothing

ADDRESS
17 Rue Vieille-du-Temple, 4th
TELEPHONE
01.48.04.82.34
METRO
Hôtel de Ville
OPEN
11AM to 6:30PM, Mon;
10:30AM to 7:30PM, Tue-Sat
CREDIT CARDS
V MC AE
$$

I was alerted to this small but bustling operation when a young Parisian friend insisted it was one of her favorite shops. And why not? Each time she passes by she thumbs through new arrivals from designers like Lolita Bis, Guy Laroche, and Max Mara, nearly always finding something worthwhile for at least 40 percent off.

The very knowledgeable and helpful saleswomen will give you their best effort even if they don't speak English. Labels are out, but they'll tell you the designer. Savings can be incredible.

JO GOLDENBERG
Delicatessen

ADDRESS
7 Rue des Rosiers, 4th
TELEPHONE
01.48.87.20.16
METRO
Saint-Paul
OPEN
9AM to 11PM daily; closed Yom Kippur
CREDIT CARDS
V, MC
$$

This popular landmark delicatessen marks the heart of Paris' oldest Jewish quarter, where kosher butchers and bakers now trade alongside Moroccan fast fooderies and high-fashion outlets. If you're longing for a *plat du jour* (about 7F) of *boulettes grandmère* (chopped meatballs) or *chou farcie* (cabbage rolls) while you read the Jewish dailies, this is your place.

ADDRESS
75 Rue Vieille-du-Temple, 3rd
TELEPHONE
01.48.87.76.18
METRO
Saint-Paul
OPEN
9AM to 6PM, Mon-Sat
CREDIT CARDS
V, AE
$$-$$$

8. ARTIS FLORA

Tapestry reproductions

The tapestries, hanging from the white walls and wood beams of what was a 17th-century home, are meant to be lifted into the present. With great success the Artis Flora workshops outside Paris recreate famous medieval and renaissance tapestries found in the Cluny Museum and in the Louvre, working each piece individually and by hand. The process involves silkscreening onto a fabric woven of flax, cotton, and wool, capturing the color intensity of the original in its current condition and guaranteeing no fading.

Cushion covers decorated with forest animals, tapestries of hunting scenes and castle life can transform a living room into a "great hall," or add romance to a bedroom. The smallest cushions begin at 300F, and are easily packed as are small rolled-up tapestries. Tapestries can get quite large and Artis Flora is well versed in shipping. Be sure to ask for their beautiful and explicit order catalog.

Artis Flora

9. LOLITA LEMPICKA
Women's clothing

Don't imagine for a moment that in Lempicka's clothes you'll be dressed for market day in Krakow. This popular designer dresses the coquette, which explains why the tailored suits are as appealing as the play clothes. Fun is the essential ingredient, with a dash of vibrant color, lots of shape, and a bit of this and that from the fabric grab bag. Lolita's look doesn't come cheap, but LOLITA BIS (across the street from the main store) is made for younger pocketbooks. At STUDIO LOLITA you'll find leftovers from both lines at half price.

ADDRESS
13 Bis Rue Pavée, 4th
ADDRESS
15 Rue Pavée, 4th (bridal)
TELEPHONE
01.42.74.50.48

ADDRESS
2 Bis Rue des Rosiers, 4th (Studio Lolita)
TELEPHONE
01.48.87.09.67
METRO
Saint-Paul

ADDRESS
14 Rue du Faubourg St-Honoré, 8th
TELEPHONE
01.49.24.94.01
METRO
Concorde

ADDRESS
46 Avenue Victor Hugo, 16th
TELEPHONE
01.45.02.14.46
OPEN
10:30AM to 7PM, Mon-Sat
CREDIT CARDS
V, AE, MC, DC
$$$$ (Lolita Lempicka), $$$ (Lolita Bis),
$$ (Studio Lolita)

10. A L'IMAGE DU GRENIER SUR L'EAU
Vintage postcards and papers

A casual browse can last hours here, as collectors or perusers may leaf through over 20,000 post cards from 1939 to the present amassed by brothers Sylvain and Yves Di Maria. If you don't have all day, you are advised to come in with a theme in mind, and the friendly brothers (they speak English) will pull the postcards on your topic from hundreds of well-organized drawers.

You can request in hushed tones something really wicked for your dressing room or a proper gift for your attorney. Prices begin at 30F and attain levels the connoisseur will certainly understand.

ADDRESS
45 Rue des Francs-Bourgeois, 4th
TELEPHONE
01.42.71.02.31
METRO
Saint-Paul
OPEN
10:30AM to 7PM, Mon-Fri;
11AM to 12:30PM & 2 to 7PM Sat
NO CREDIT CARDS
$-$$$

ADDRESS
17 Rue des Francs-Bourgeois, 4th
TELEPHONE
01.42.72.04.00
METRO
Saint-Paul
OPEN
10AM to 1PM & 2 to 7PM, Mon-Fri & Sun; 10AM to 7PM, Sat
CREDIT CARDS
V MC
$$

11. JEAN-PIERRE DE CASTRO

Antique silver and silverplate tableware

If you long to complete your dining service with the family silver, but have none, you'll find history altered here. Begin with baskets full of silverplated flatware, worn but not weary, whose past life was likely as a hotel service, selling for 400F/kilo (about 15 pieces).

Move on to the pure silver and choose from among hundreds of forks, knives, and spoons engraved Christofle and the like, that earned their rich patina at the tables of fine French homes, sold here at prices comparable to new silverplate at Christofle. Then turn to coffee and tea services, serving platters, and small accessory items that make wonderful wedding gifts.

The breadth of design and origin of these pieces allows you to set the palace table or bistro kitchen. Inventory here spans the 18th, 19th, and 20th centuries. Let the smiling and patient sales help explain to you how to date French silver by the markings on the back side. Plan to pack or mail your purchases as M. de Castro does not handle shipping.

Jean-Pierre de Castro

12. MEUBLES PEINTS
Painted wooden furniture

The popular painted armoires and chests that warm this shop are transformed from tired and faceless cast-offs of 18th- and 19th-century households to splendid pieces of hand-painted country furniture.

Jean-Pierre Besenval retrieves much from the Alsacian countryside, working behind his shopfront to individually restore and color each piece with egg-tempura motifs borrowed from the brightly decorative traditions of eastern France, Swiss baroque style, the Italian renaissance, and the Black Forest. Whether you choose a blanket chest (from 8,000F) to cheer up a dreary corner or an armoire (from 16,000F) to anchor an entire room, you'll appreciate its individuality in a home setting. The shop obligingly handles shipping for its many foreign customers.

ADDRESS
32 Rue Sévigné, 4th
TELEPHONE
01.42.77.54.60
METRO
Saint-Paul
OPEN
Noon to 7PM, Tue-Sun
NO CREDIT CARDS
$$$

13. CARNAVALETTE
Vintage prints and engravings, newspapers, magazines

"Carnavalette" is the pet name Mme de Sévigné called her residence, now the Musée Carnavalette. And this shop is a fond haunt for both amateur and serious collectors of 19th-century printed works. The 22-year-old establishment is run by cousins who specialize in the amusing work of Sem, the favorite caracaturist of high society during the *belle époque*.

In their well-organized stacks you'll find nicely detailed fashion prints, engravings of the city of Paris, maps, and publications such as *Gil Blas*, popular for its black humor (50F for an 1896 edition in good shape).

ADDRESS
2 Rue des Francs-Bourgeois, 3rd
TELEPHONE
01.42.72.91.92
METRO
Saint-Paul
OPEN
10:30AM to 6:30PM, every day
NO CREDIT CARDS
$$

Carnavalette

Along the Way

The PLACE DES VOSGES is a beautifully symmetrical park surrounded by 36 slate-roofed, limestone townhouses. The oldest square in Paris (it was commissioned by Henry IV in the 1600s) has benefited from its restoration as centerpiece to the neighborhood.

Once again an aristocracy of intellectuals and artists compete to claim an address on the former PLACE ROYALE. A traditional spot to enjoy the architecture and activity is the café MA BOURGOGNE (N.19 Place des Vosges), where you can relax outdoors with a café au lait in the company of locals and well-known customers such as Inspector Maigret from the Simenon detective novels.

Stroll under the arcades to view the luxurious lingerie at FANNY LIAUTARD (N.2) next to her white wedding gowns, and on to the geometric day and night designs for the geometric body at POPY MORENI (N.13).

ADDRESS
24 Place des Vosges, 3rd
TELEPHONE
01.42.77.61.90
METRO
Saint-Paul
OPEN
2 to 6:30PM, Tue-Sat
CREDIT CARDS
V
$$-$$$$

14. JARDIN DE FLORE

Limited edition prints

This spacious publishing house-gallery produces its own deluxe re-editions from a huge variety of 17th- and 18th-century illustrations, maps and books whose originals are in the Louvre. Employing traditional handmade papers, hand-coloring techniques and renaissance bookbinding methods, the house creates reproductions at least as worthy as the now-worn originals.

The extraordinary colorwork and attention to detail have drawn the patronage of former President Mitterand, who ordered a pair of three-foot world globes for his office. By request you will have excellent service in this often busy shop, and are sure to carry out something that will last a century or so. Be sure to peek at the art nouveau doorway achieved in acrylic by jeweler Jean Filhos.

15. ANDRE BISSONNET

Antique musical instruments

M. Bissonet began restoring antique musical instruments in the cold-storage room of his butcher's
shop. When the instruments took over he packed away
his cleavers, took off his apron, and hung a musician's
sign over the butcher's plaque. Impassioned with the
near-extinct instruments of the 17th, 18th, and 19th
centuries, the engaging proprietor can explain them
all, play many, and restores them to perfection. Even if
you don't leave with a 17th-century harp, your visit
here will be fascinating.

ADDRESS
6 Rue Pas-de-la-Mule, 3rd
TELEPHONE
01.48.87.20.15
METRO
Bastille
OPEN
2 to 7PM, Mon-Sat; mornings
by appointment; closed August
NO CREDIT CARDS
$$$

16. OBJET INSOLITE

Hardware and fixtures

Whether you prefer doorknobs that ressemble jewel-
encrusted daggers or bronze snail shells, you'll find
objects of unusual beauty in this gallery dedicated to
household fixtures that are objects of art. The pieces
here are commissioned from respected names in design
(among them are Migeon & Migeon, Garouste &
Bonetti, Kalinger) and reproduced in limited quanti-
ties. Come here for a mirror that's not a mirror, a star-
tling lamp, an ingenious dish or vase. While the inven-
tory changes frequently, you're bound to find some-
thing magical that will fit into your luggage.

ADDRESS
109 Blvd Beaumarchais, 3rd
TELEPHONE
01.42.71.30.94
METRO
St-Sébastien Froissart
OPEN
10AM to 12:30PM & 1:30 to
7PM, Tue-Fri; closes at 5PM
Mon; noon to 7PM, Sat
CREDIT CARDS
V
$$$

ADDRESS
13 Rue de Turenne, 4th
TELEPHONE
01.42.78.77.00
METRO
Saint-Paul
OPEN
11:30AM to 7PM, Tue-Sat;
closed the last week in July
until September
NO CREDIT CARDS
$$

17. L'ARLEQUIN
Antique glassware and crystal

If I were a newlywed, L'Arlequin would be my first stop after acquiring my silver at J. P. de Castro. The glassware (on the right side of the shop) and crystal (on the left) here is exclusively French 19th-century or earlier, kept on rather dimly lit floor-to-ceiling shelves by the devoted owner Dominique Ronot.

This is where the French come to round out or replace extinct family patterns, or simply to pick up something old and beautiful for the table. Baccarat and Saint-Louis from the last century are offered at 300 to 400F a glass, with decanters from 800F. There are unique pieces or sets from village engravers who would blow and etch glasses especially to commemorate village festivals, and romantic pairs of champagne flutes in the straight-sided designs of past centuries.

Mme Ronot won't handle shipping but she will package your purchases in a carryon carton for the plane or point you toward a shipper.

ADDRESS
Enter at 14-15 Rue Saint-Paul,
4th
METRO
Saint-Paul
OPEN
Noon to 7PM, Mon & Thurs-
Sun
CREDIT CARDS
Accepted by some dealers
$-$$$

18. VILLAGE SAINT-PAUL
Antiques shops

This warren of antiques dealers and *brocanteurs* (sellers of bric-a-brac) tucked away in the courtyard between the Rue Saint-Paul and the Rue Charlemagne is perhaps the most charming antiques hunting ground in Paris, and a favorite among my Parisian friends.

The 60-odd dealers trade in everything from fine antiques to Grandmère's costume jewelry, with plenty of personality to liven up a serious search. Be sure not to miss GLORIA D'HIER (N.15 Rue Saint-Paul) for 19th-century pewter and table services, and the shops on the Rue Saint-Paul. A perfect afternoon in the village should include a simple lunch in the courtyard or an ethnic bite nearby.

The Sixteenth

After you've chased the charm and history down each cobblestone street, seen the sights and bumped into too many tourists, it's time to retreat to the sedate 16th for an afternoon of shopping that is reliably calm, comfortable, and conservative, in the neighborhood that the *haute bourgeoisie* discreetly calls home. The impeccable *fin-de-siècle* residences that line these streets shelter the *BCBG (Bon Chic Bon Genre)*, the Parisian equivalent of the preppy, born and bred to carry on the values of that class. Leaving nothing to chance, the *Rallye* (coming out) of Mlle BCBG is a five-year process, and the young man she will eventually marry has likely attended one of the prestigious prep schools in the neighborhood.

In this primarily residential district you'll find an unhurried and uncrowded kind of shopping, with quiet neighborhood branches of many of the city's best boutiques, and resale shops of the highest caliber. Take a stroll down the elegant boulevard AVENUE VICTOR-HUGO where many well-know fashion designers have shops offering their more conservative styles and attentive service to those who choose to shop in this neighborhood: start with these names: GUY LAROCHE, N.9; JEAN-LOUIS SCHERRER, N.14; SAINT-LAURENT RIVE GAUCHE, N.19; GIVENCHY, N.66, to name just a few.

You'll find more fashion on the nearby RUE DE PASSY, as well as two worthwhile standbys: the department store that tastefully clothes women of the neighborhood, FRANCK ET FILS (N.80), only crowded during its sensational sales in January and July; and SEPHORA (N.50), which offers hundreds of beauty products, perfumes, and cosmetics to the same *"soignée"* (well-groomed) crowd. Then there are the sidestreets, which shouldn't be ignored. All in all, the 16th is among the most pleasant shopping areas in Paris, and if you are disposed toward the BCBG life, you'll love it here.

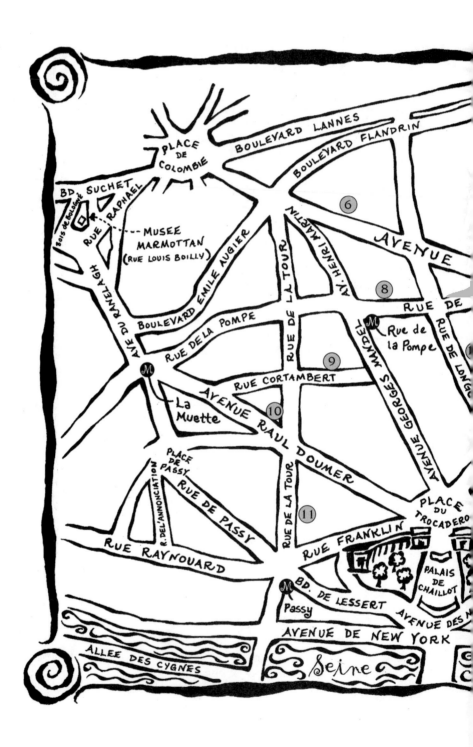

Where to Stay

SAINT JAMES CLUB

ADDRESS
43 Avenue de Bugeaud, 16th
TELEPHONE
01.44.05.81.81
FAX
01.44.05.81.82
METRO
Porte Dauphine or Victor-Hugo
Double rooms from 1750F
CREDIT CARDS
V, AE, MC

The only *château*-like hotel in Paris, the St-James club is a unique opportunity for visitors wanting to experience *la vie au château* (chateau life). Once a home for visiting scholars, the magnificent library is now the setting for the piano bar in this altogether elegant establishment. Rooms are done in a luxurious '30s style, and there is a health club on the premises. The park-like grounds are open only to hotel guests and to members of the exclusive St-James Club.

HOTEL PERGOLESE

ADDRESS
3 Rue Pergolèse, 16th
TELEPHONE
01.40.67.96.77
FAX
01.45.00.12.11
METRO
Argentine
Double rooms from 950F
CREDIT CARDS
V, AE, MC

A deluxe boutique hotel with first-rate service and amenities, this is a well-priced choice for those who appreciate elegant modern decor. Pale, uncluttered spaces defined by glass block and wall panels and filled with light ash and leather furnishings were designed by Rena Dumas, known for her adventurous interiors.

HOTEL ETOILE-MAILLOT

ADDRESS
10 Rue du Bois de Boulogne, corner of Rue Duret (16th)
TELEPHONE
01.45.00.42.60
FAX
01.45.00.55.89
METRO
Argentine, Charles-de-Gaulle Etoile
Double rooms from 600F;
Breakfast included
CREDIT CARDS
V, AE, MC

You'll feel you're staying in a fine French home a few blocks from the Bois when you check in here. The antique furnishings from the periods of Louis XV & XVI and the opulent fabrics benefit from an attentive staff, and so do the guests.

Culture Along the Way

MUSEE MARMOTTAN

This quiet and intimate gem tucked away from the crowds contains the premier collection of Monet's work, including his *Waterlilies*, also enjoy other impressionists and medieval illuminated manuscripts. Open 10AM to 5:30PM, Tue-Sun.

ADDRESS
2 Rue Louis-Boilly, 16th
METRO
La Muette

BOIS DE BOLOGNE

The Bois is the top destination for nature-loving Parisians. Rent a bike here and explore over 2,000 acres of lakes, gardens, restaurants, and the delightful JARDIN D'ACCLIMATATION (children's amusement park/zoo). The tulips, roses, and water lilies in the Parc de Bagatelle are not to be missed. Open 9AM to 10PM, summer; 9AM to 5:30PM, winter.

METRO
Porte Dauphine or Porte D'Auteil

The Sixteenth Shops

ADDRESS
4 Place d'Iéna, 16th
TELEPHONE
01.40.70.14.63
METRO
Iéna
OPEN
10AM to 7PM, Mon-Sat
CREDIT CARDS
V, AE
$$$

1. NOEL
Household linens

This centenarian house carries on the tradition of delicate and sumptuous linens, maintaining its reputation as seamstress of some of the world's most beautiful table services of the organdy hand-embroidered sort (5,000-20,000F). Though the number of households in need of such refinement may seem to be dwindling, Noel has 12,000 embroidery designs in its archives, sustained by an international customer list with a strong following in the States. In the same tradition are embroidered table sets, bed linens, and toweling (a stitched guest towel makes a gift possible at 200F).

For those who live in the modern world, Noel has taken a step in time and now offers T-shirts with truly wonderful embroideries of birds, hats, pencils, and the like at a reasonable 400F.

Noel

2. CÉLINE
Women's clothing and leather goods

For that BCBG look that can be nothing other than Parisian, Céline is it. You'll find the finest quality leather goods (shoes, belts, and handbags) in the classic, gold-trimmed tradition of Chanel and Hermès, without quite the same price tags. Upstairs is a collection of day and evening wear exhibiting the same stylish good taste.

This should be your first stop for the leather skirt, silk blouse, and metal-buttoned sweater that look so appropriate while shopping the sixteenth.

ADDRESS
3 Avenue Victor-Hugo, 16th
TELEPHONE
01.45.01.80.01
METRO
Etoile or Victor-Hugo

ADDRESS
24 Rue François 1er, 8th
TELEPHONE
01.47.20.14.33
METRO
Alma-Marçeau

ADDRESS
58 Rue de Rennes, 6th
TELEPHONE
01.45.48.5.8.55
METRO
Rennes
OPEN
10AM to 7PM, Mon-Sat
CREDIT CARDS
V, AE, MC
$$$-$$$$

3. POINT A LA LIGNE
Decorative candles

An extraordinary collection of *trompe l'oeil* centerpiece candles lights up any style table and perfume the air about. From a potted cactus or mushroom to a life-size purple hyacinth growing out of a bulb, to a fragrant and abundant bouquet (140F), these still lifes in wax are designed to tease and please the sensibilities of your guests.

Depending upon the occasion, choose between a formal row of miniature orange trees or the giant pumpkin. Coordinating paper plates, cloths, and napkins are also available.

ADDRESS
7 Avenue Victor Hugo, 16th
TELEPHONE
01.45.00.96.80
METRO
Victor Hugo or Kléber
OPEN
10AM to 7PM, Mon-Sat
CREDIT CARDS
V, AE, DC
$$

ADDRESS
49 Avenue Victor Hugo, 16th
TELEPHONE
01.45.02.21.21
METRO
Victor-Hugo
OPEN
9AM to 9PM, every day

ADDRESS
44 Rue du Bac, 7th
TELEPHONE
01.42.22.39.39
METRO
Rue du Bac
OPEN
9AM to 8PM, Mon-Sat & 9AM to
1PM, Sun
CREDIT CARDS
V, MC
$$

4. LENOTRE
Pasteries, candies, breads, prepared dishes

For inspiration at home, I keep a glossy fold-out of Lenotre's *Merveilles de Patisseries* (Pastry Marvels) on my fridge. Gaston Lenotre is known worldwide for such lucious and lyrical cakes as Mozart (gooseberries, Grand Marnier, and meringue) and Opera (almond cake, coffee mousse, and chocolate truffle) as well as for his candies, ice creams, decorated bread loaves, salads, and entrées.

He has nine branches in Paris alone, and each lives up to his reputation, though those listed at left may be most convenient. At lunchtime, stop in for a delicious carry-out sandwich. The Victor-Hugo shop is larger, and if you peek at the window displays, you won't be able to pass by without stopping in for at least a bag of candies.

ADDRESS
116 Avenue Victor Hugo, 16th
TELEPHONE
01.44.05.18.08
FAX
01.44.05.07.01
METRO
Victor-Hugo
OPEN
10AM to 7PM, Mon-Sat
CREDIT CARDS
V, AE, MC
$$$

5. LE DUC DU PRASLIN
Chocolates

If you require pralines (chocolaty concoctions garnished with caramelized almonds) as I do, you'll be pleased to have this address. Not only can you stock up on beautifully presented bonbons while you're here, but in the gourmand tradition you can pick up a catalog and fax your orders from home.

The management recommends a minimum 2-kilo purchase for the best postal value, with a cost of about 200F for airmail special delivery within 10 days. A little bag of 20 grams worth of pralines is 23F, and it goes up from there. Also worth your while are the *grelons* (caramelized hazelnuts in milk chocolate and powdered sugar) and *givrettes* (almonds given the same treatment). The exotic assortment of filled chocolates is both exhaustive and delicious.

Le Duc du Praslin

6. LA CHÂTELAINE
Children's clothing, household linens

Every indulgent *grandmère* in Paris knows that La Châtelaine will have the appropriate dresses, shawls, baptismal gowns and gifts for their newest family member, and will outfit him/her in *Bon Chic Bon Genre* style to age 12.

European royalty come here for the hand-sewn collection exclusive to this shop, and the house seamstresses will fit a garment for your prince or princess at no extra charge. The lace pillowcases, embroidered bath towels, and organdy table sets are also fit for a princess, but accessible to regular customers during the store's very favorable sales.

ADDRESS
170 Avenue Victor Hugo, 16th
TELEPHONE
01.47.27.44.07
METRO
Pompe
OPEN
9;30AM to 6:30PM, Tue-Fri;
9:30AM to 12:30PM & 2:30 to
6:30PM, Sat
CREDIT CARDS
V, MC
$$$-$$$$

7. JOHN DEMERSAY
CHARLES BOSQUET
Men's and women's tailored clothing

Both these handsome shops are stocked by Arthur & Fox, a French company whose tailoring savvy leans toward the English tradition. Particularly at the end of the workday, they are bustling with smartly dressed customers who stop off to replenish their office wardrobes with classically cut suits in seasonable tweeds, linens, and silks, and fine cotton shirts (from 400F), which the excellent sales staff will help you put together with a *savoir-faire* that is distinctly French. Shirts and suits are also made-to-measure (suits from 6,000F).

But what may interest you even more than the reasonable prices and solid styling is that these stores welcome an order-by-mail clientele.

JOHN DEMERSAY
ADDRESS
133 Rue de la Pompe, 16th
TELEPHONE
01.45.53.05.15
METRO
Victor-Hugo

CHARLES BOSQUET
ADDRESS
13 Rue Marbeuf, 8th
TELEPHONE
01.47.20.65.59
METRO
Franklin D. Roosevelt
OPEN
9:30AM to 7PM, Mon-Sat
CREDIT CARDS
V, AE, MC
$$

ADDRESS
89 Rue de la Pompe
(Housewares and gifts)

ADDRESS
92-93&95 Rue de la Pompe,
16th (Women's and children's
clothing)

ADDRESS
101 Rue de la Pompe
(Menswear)

ADDRESS
123 Rue de la Pompe
(Outerwear)
TELEPHONE
01.42.04.30.28
METRO
Pompe
OPEN
11AM to 7:30PM, Tue-Sat
CREDIT CARDS
V, AE, MC
$$

8. RÉCIPROQUE
Resale designer clothing and gifts

Don't mistake this establishment for a mere neighborhood resale shop, though it most certainly reflects the *bon ton* that is the 16th. In a city where some simply cannot be seen in the same couture threads twice, Réciproque has brought respectability, high standards and high style to the secondhand clothing trade.

On any business day you'll find the row of boutiques brisk with customers cruising the racks for this year's Ungaro gown, a Hermès scarf, a Cartier bag. The 30,000 or so fashionable items here are in immaculate condition and at least 50 percent less than when brand new. You'll notice that those who come to consign their clothing (perhaps a diplomat, a banker's wife, a student) leave with their bags as full as when they came in.

ADDRESS
18 Rue Cortambert, 16th
TELEPHONE
01.45.03.15.55
METRO
Pompe
OPEN
11AM to 1PM & 2 to 7PM, Mon-Sat
CREDIT CARDS
V, AE, MC
$$$$

9. CHRISTIAN BENAIS
Antique linens

Residents of the 16th who don't care to scour the flea markets for their antique linens rely on the good taste of Christian Benais to present them with the best finds in his lovely and well-patronized shop.

Decorator par excellence, Benais caters to appreciative customers who come here for the exquisite selection of decorative pillow shams trimmed in lace, embroideries, and antique prints; embroidered table services (from 3,500F); and bedspreads of his own design among classic linens and decorative accessories geared to the stylishly traditional homes of the neighborhood.

CARRETTE

Tea salon

ADDRESS
4 Place du Trocadéro, 16th
TELEPHONE
01.47.27.88.56
METRO
Trocadéro
OPEN
8AM to 7PM, Mon & Wed-Sun
(closed August)
Hot meals served until 4PM
NO CARDS
$$

A terrace table at this spacious tea salon is just the place to make a thorough study of the look and habits of the BCBG. Plant yourself here for a mid-morning chocolate and pastry and watch the world go by, or stay for the lively lunch hours.

10. LES FOLIES D'ELODIE

Women's lingerie and evening wear

Since she opened, the exclusive Elodie label has caused a sensation. Simple but sexy dinner suits and evening gowns as well as some of Paris's most luxurious lingerie and sleepwear are seen in these sister shops, run by sisters.

Lingerie is done in silk satins, Calais lace, and microfibers, all sewn exclusively for the Elodie label, in a look so alluring that many of the customers buying lingerie here are men buying for women. The Elodie workshop allows clients to choose from a wide range of fabrics and color, any standard style to be made up at no extra cost, ready for pickup or shipping in ten days. The Paul-Doumer store is the larger of the two, and merchandise can vary between them.

ADDRESS
56 Avenue Paul-Doumer, 16th
TELEPHONE
01.45.04.93.57
METRO
La Muette

LES NUITS D'ELODIE

ADDRESS
1 Bis Avenue MacMahon, 17th
TELEPHONE
01.42.27.94.22
METRO
Etoile
OPEN
10AM to 7PM, Tue-Sat
CREDIT CARDS
V, AE, MC
$$$-$$$$

Address
14-16 Rue de la Tour, 16th
(Women's)
TELEPHONE
01.45.20.95.21
25 Rue de la Tour, 16th (Men's)
TELEPHONE
01.45.27.11.46
METRO
Passy
OPEN
2 to 7PM, Mon; 10AM to 7PM,
Tue-Sat
CREDIT CARDS
V, MC
$$

11. DEPOT-VENTE DE PASSY
Designer resale and overstock clothing

Catherine Baril's resale shop of the stars and accompanying designer overstock handles only those items from the top designers (yes, you can also find accessories from Hermès, Chanel, and YSL) in top condition, and at prices any budget could bear.

ADDRESS
100 Rue de Longchamps, 16th
(Children and adults)
TELEPHONE
01.47.27.91.53
METRO
Pompe

ADDRESS
5 Rue des Cannettes, 6th
(Children and adults)
TELEPHONE
01.43.54.75.25
METRO
Mabillon
OPEN
10AM to 7PM (to 7:30 in 6th),
Mon-Sat
CREDIT CARDS
V, AE, MC
$$

12. NAF-NAF
Children's, junior, adult clothes

The Naf-Naf line, named after the youngest of the Three Little Pigs, experienced instant success with its first design: a very wide, printed jumpsuit, now much-copied. Even though it calls itself the "big, bad look," the casual collection is identifiable by its gay colors and shapes, and is most popular with teenagers.

Naf-Naf

Paris on a Budget

The shops of Paris are a feast for the eyes, but untempered indulgence can mean famine for the pocketbook. While the French themselves always appear so stylish and seem to consider window-shopping an appropriate national pasttime, the tourist may well wonder how it's possible for the average wage-earner to play the part without going broke.

The typical *Parisienne* is a smart and seasoned shopper on a budget. She is used to window-shopping for ideas, then going to buy where she knows she'll get the best price.

Keep in mind that virtually every store has a major sale during the first three weeks of January and in July. Two notable exceptions are the weeklong October sale at HERMÈS, and the March and October sales at the department stores GALERIES LAFAYETTE and PRINTEMPS. For the tourist, shopping at these *grands magasins* offers the maximum variety in merchandise to achieve the *détaxe* minimum of purchases totaling over 1,200F, and simplifies the reimbursement process. Before you shop here, go to the Welcome Desk for an additional 10 percent discount card available to tourists upon presentation of passport.

Keep your eyes open for the words *Soldes* (a sale is taking place), *Fin de Séries* (end of the collection), *Dégriffés* (labels cut out), *Stock* (overstock), or *Dépot Vente* (resale establishment) for good values year-round.

Many style-conscious yet budget-minded haunts have already been metioned in this book. Here's where else the smart shopper goes:

Clothing and Household

MONOPRIX and PRISUNIC are mini-department stores offering clothing, accessories, groceries, and household items at low prices, with locations throughout the city. They are extremely well merchandised (Monoprix is owned by Galeries Lafayette and Prisunic by the Printemps department store). Everyone shops at these stores: even Princess Stephanie has been seen at Monoprix rounding out her wardrobe. Here are some convenient locations:

MONOPRIX

ADDRESS
1 Avenue de L'Opéra, 1st
TELEPHONE
01.42.61.78.08
METRO
Havre-Caumartin
OPEN
9AM to 8PM, Mon-Wed & Fri-Sat; 9AM to 9PM, Thurs.
CREDIT CARDS
V, MC

Parisiennes come here for the Bourjois cosmetics line, which is Chanel makeup under a different label at very low prices. They buy their children's clothes here, their hair accessories, and understated separates to put with their couture label jackets.

PRISUNIC

ADDRESS
52 Avenue des Champs-Elysées, 8th
TELEPHONE
01.42.25.27.46
METRO
Franklin-D-Roosevelt
OPEN
9:45AM to midnight, Mon-Sat
CREDIT CARDS
V, MC

This crowded scene nevertheless offers good gift buys on the off-hours. Latch onto a shopping cart and grab up some "typically French" items like kitchen gadgets or Provençal pottery. As a student I made some wardrobe purchases here that continued to draw compliments 10 years later.

Discount Clothing Areas

If you're an experienced bargain-basement shopper, you won't be put off by the crowds or lack of service in some of these shops (Rue d'Alésia is more civilized than Saint-Placide). The ambiance is virtually nil, changing rooms in short supply, but discounts hover around 40-50 percent of original prices.

RUE D'ALÉSIA, 14TH

Rue d'Alésia boutiques offer last season's designer fashions at great prices but in an inconvenient location. While you're here, you should stop at SR (N.64) for Sonia Rykiel's timeless knits and velours of past seasons; DOROTHEE BIS STOCK (N.74) for sportswear and tennis attire from this fashionable designer, accepts Visa; STOCK 2 (N.92) for Daniel Hechter collection ends for men, women, and children, no credit cards; FABRICE KAREL STOCK (N.105) for classic knits, accepts Visa; KOOKAI (#111) for the kooky looks that teenage girls adore, no credit cards; and CACHAREL STOCK (N.114) for truly wearable Parisian style.

METRO
Alésia
CREDIT CARDS
Accepted by some shops
OPEN
10AM to 7PM Tue-Sat, 2 to 7PM, Mon; closed August

RUE SAINT-PLACIDE, 6TH

Anything but placid, this short discount drag begins just outside the doors of the department store Bon Marché, and if you're persistent, insistant, and under 35, you're bound to find something quite up-to-the-minute. There are few designer labels here.

METRO
Sainte-Placide
CREDIT CARDS
Accepted by some shops

Designer Overstock

Here are two top "Designer Stock" houses not yet listed:

MENDÈS/YSL

ADDRESS
65 Rue Montmartre, 2nd
TELEPHONE
01.42.36.83.32
METRO
Sentier
OPEN
10AM to 6:30PM, Mon-Fri;
10AM to 5:30PM, Sat
CREDIT CARDS
V MC

Here in the heart of the garment district, Mendès is famous for offering last season's Christian Lacroix, and Yves Saint-Laurent's Rive Gauche (2nd floor) and Variations (main floor) collections at half price. Be forewarned that there are no private changing rooms and the salespeople won't go out of their way to help you. The collections arrive here in July and January.

SOLDE TROIS/LANVIN

ADDRESS
3 Rue de Vienne, 8th
TELEPHONE
01.42.94.93.34
METRO
Europe
OPEN
10:30AM to 1:30PM &2:30 to
6PM, Mon-Fri; 10:30AM to
2:30PM, Sat
CREDIT CARDS
V, MC

The sumptuous Lanvin collection for men and women, accessories included, is offered here at 40 percent less than what it would have cost at his Faubourg Saint-Honoré boutiques. Well-attended sales in January and June bring prices down another 50 percent!

Fabrics

LE HAMEAU COOLMAN
Designer upholstery fabrics

ADDRESS
17 Rue de la Chapelle, 18th
TELEPHONE
01.42.02.00.33
METRO
Marx-Dormoy
OPEN
10:30AM to 12:30PM & 2 to
6PM, Mon-Sat
NO CREDIT CARDS

When you've chosen your fabrics at Canovas, Etamine, and Patrick Frey, run across town to Coolman to place your orders. Fabrics from the current collections are priced at 20 to 30 percent less than at the designers' boutiques, before the *détaxe*, and Coolman will handle your shipping.

If you come here first, you can look through their fabric books and consult the in-house decorator. This large operation handles many of the big names in decorating, including their wallpapers and bed linens.

MENDES TISSUS
Designer dressmaking fabrics

If you've ever thought you (or your dressmaker) could whip up a little something that could pass for *haute couture*, given the proper fixings, come here to choose among leftover bolts of the very same fabrics cut by Yves Saint-Laurent only a few weeks before. Conveniently, winter fabrics begin to arrive in September, and summer fabrics in February.

ADDRESS
140 Rue Montmartre, 2nd
TELEPHONE
01.42.36.02.39
METRO
Bourse
OPEN
9:30AM to 6PM, Mon-Fri
CREDIT CARDS
V, MC

Table Arts

RUE DE PARADIS, 10TH

A true paradise for those who love to create a beautiful table, the rue de Paradis is lined with divine shops and showrooms paying homage to France's finest china, silver, and crystal. If you spend a few hours shopping this street, you will be able to put together the table of your dreams at prices more competitive than in the center of town, often with an additional discount for a quantity purchase. These shops can help you in English, accept credit cards, are reliable shippers, and will fill future orders sent to their fax numbers.

The highlight of the street is the BACCARAT MUSEUM across the courtyard at N.31 bis rue de Paradis, but every store here is worth looking into. Shop around for the best prices.

Be sure not to miss: LIMOGES UNIC (N.12 & N.58) for its classic porcelain pieces, in a variety of forms not always available in the U.S.; ARTS CERAMIQUES (N.15) for hand-painted earthenware (*faience*), including Quimper patterns rarely seen, and pewter table accessories that complement its rustic look; LA TISANERIE PORCELAINE (N.35) for simple white porcelain table settings and serving pieces which can be personalized with your initials or special design.

At N.18 Rue du Paradis is the Musée d'Affiche (Poster Museum), where exhibits are on view and a large and reasonably priced selection of poster reproductions is for sale.

METRO
Château d'Eau
OPEN
10AM to 6:30PM, Mon-Sat most shops
CREDIT CARDS
Accepted by some shops

Handcrafts

ARTISINAT MONASTIQUE
Embroidered linens, children's clothes, porcelaines, gifts

ADDRESS
68 Bis Avenue Denfert-
Rochereau, 14th
TELEPHONE
01.43.35.15.76
METRO
Denfert-Rochereau
OPEN
12 to 6:30PM, Mon-Fri;
2 to 7PM, Sat
CARDS
V, MC (purchases over 200F)

In the vaults of a medieval convent you'll find hand-crafts produced by monks and nuns living in cloisters throughout France. At prices that are quite reasonable you can take home beautiful hand or machine embroidered bed and table linens, or custom order monograms or special patterns, stationery printed to specification, and you'll be enchanted by little dresses embellished by loving hands, handmade books, painted porcelains, and gift items from this very special provenance.

VIADUCT DES ARTS

ADDRESS
9-129, Avenue Daumesnil, 12th
TELEPHONE
01.44.75.80.66
METRO
Ledru-Rollin
OPEN
Mon-Fri
CREDIT CARDS
Accepted by some shops

Here in the Faubourg St-Antoine, hub of the fine furniture industry since the 17th-century, city planners have revitalized an abandoned train viaduct by creating workshops and display for master craftspeople underneath a mile-long stretch of brick arches, and a planted promenade for strollers on top. The array of talents here is dazzling, showcasing the most skilled artisans representing a balance of the crafts.

Begin at ATELIERS DE LA SOURCE (N. 9 Avenue Daumesnil) for fine cabinetry with an emphasis on inlay of 18th-century designs; GALERIE V.I.A. (N.29-37) houses the best of the modern movement under one roof: furniture, lighting, and accessories by the country's most innovative designers; at BAGUES (N.73), the 156-year-old firm who has remade chandeliers for Versailles, you can purchase a sconce fit for a queen for about 1,500F. Keep exploring, you'll find centuries' worth of home improvements under the viaduct's 60 arches.

Flea Markets

A trip to the *marché aux puces* (flea market), that very French shopping experience, can be a welcome contrast to the luxury and prices of the city boutiques. Be sure to arrive early, because there is lots of competition for the better items.

Put on your most comfortable walking shoes and your drabbest attire if you intend to go far. Looking too glamourous can put a damper on the discount you may be able to secure—up to 30 percent off if you're really expert. Keep in mind that you have no protection against purchasing reproductions or fraudulent pieces, other than your own probing questions. The seller who responds that he doesn't know the answer is probably hiding something.

For a piece over 100 years old be sure to get a certificate of authenticity to avoid customs duty. Most dealers will help arrange shipping, which may seem high, so be sure to factor in your estimated savings by purchasing directly in France.

MARCHE AUX PUCES DE SAINT-OUEN (CLIGNANCOURT FLEA MARKET)
Antiques and secondhand furnishings and clothing

ADDRESS
Porte de Clignancourt/Saint-Ouen, 18th
METRO
Porte de Clignancourt
OPEN
7AM to 6PM, Sat, Sun, Mon; dealers only on Friday mornings
CREDIT CARDS
Accepted by some dealers; bring traveler's checks or cash
$-$$$$

Welcome to Les Puces, where you can rummage through centuries of discards from farmhouse attics and *châteaux*, along with Parisian housewives, tourists and discerning dealers from around the world. A trip here is always fun and you're certain to find a treasure to take home, though a true find is rare.

If you have professional credentials, you will be allowed in on Friday mornings (dealers' day) when the bargains are bought up and the most important pieces change hands. Typically, prices at Les Puces run about 20 percent lower than in Paris. By Tuesday you can be sure that the best merchandise will be marked up for resale in a fancy antique shop on the Left Bank or St-Honoré.

Located just outside the city limits of Paris, in the town of St-Ouen, this is the largest antiques/flea market in the world, and much too big to cover in a day. Once the business address of a handful of ragpickers anxious to avoid city taxes on their sales, Clignancourt now has 3,000 saavy dealers working from permanent stands and portable tables.

The market center, where the better stalls are located, is a several-block walk from the metro station, heading north on the Avenue Clignancourt (under the Périphérique), and turning left on the Rue des Rosiers. As you continue up this street you'll find separate markets on either side, each with a distinct personality and packed with individually owned stalls. Guides to the stalls and their specialties are sold at the information booths at the markets Biron, Paul-Bert, and Vernaison.

The following are your best bets:

The large and eclectic MARCHE VERNAISON (N.99 Rue des Rosiers and 136 Rue Michelet) sells small collectibles, linens, porcelains, and art deco knickknacks. Keep your eyes open for landscapes, still lifes and ancestral portraits, which can go for a song when the artist is an unknown.

MARCHE BIRON and its annex MARCHE CAMBO (N.85 and N.75 Rue des Rosiers) deal in genuine antiques priced to impress, from rare furniture and Napoleonic objects to beautiful old dolls (Stand 50, Biron), early posters (Stand 137, Biron), perfect 19th-century table services (Stand 142, Biron) and antique lace (Stand 153, Biron).

MARCHE SERPETTE (N.110 Rue des Rosiers) is *très à la mode* with its specialty in pieces from 1900 to 1960.

MARCHE PAUL BERT (N.104 Rue des Rosiers and N.18 Rue Paul Bert) is the favorite of American buyers, full of affordable and stylish items in a charming setting. After you've chosen your gilt mirror and bathroom chandelier, mix with the young dealers over lunch at LE RESTAURANT PAUL BERT (N.20 Rue Paul Bert), or in the *belle époque* decor of CHEZ LOUISETTE (N.130 Avenue Michelet). Whether or not you cook at home, don't miss BACHELIER ANTIQUITÉS (Allé 1, Stand 17), where Bachelier mother and son preside over gadgets for the kitchen, each an eye-catching bit of nostalgia guaranteed to be in working order.

MARCHE JULES-VALLES (N.17 Rue Jules-Valles) offers the least serious and least expensive shopping experience at Clignancourt. Here you can enjoy a good dicker over the price of countless curios with a dying breed of *brocanteurs* (secondhand dealers).

MARCHE MALIK (N.60 Rue Jules-Valles) is famous for its *fripes* (vintage clothing) and its pickpockets. Keep your francs well guarded throughout this excursion.

MARCHEE AUX PUCES DE VANVES
Collectibles and small antiques

ADDRESS
Avenues Georges-Lafenestre et Marc Sangnier, 14th
METRO
Porte de Vanves
OPEN
8AM to 12PM, Sat & Sun
NO CREDIT CARDS
$$

Small and convenient, Vanves offers a good alternative to Clignancourt. It can be fully inspected in two hours and is located just a few minutes from central Paris. Early Saturday mornings (better pickings than Sunday), is the best time to make the easy trip to this newly fashionable flea market.

You can uncover a choice pair of silver candlesticks, a bolt of ornate antique fabric, antique toys, 19th-century prints, and unusual furniture pieces at good prices.

This is the stuff of the *brocanteur,* somewhere between unusual antiques and collectible junk. The best dealers pull up shop at lunchtime and a group of true junk dealers moves in.

When you've had enough, go next door to the old books market in the PARK GEORGES BRASSENS. Every Sunday morning from March to October the SQUARE GEORGE-LAFENESTRE becomes an open-air gallery, where you can buy paintings and sculpture directly from the artists.

Shop Talk

The following are translations of many French words and phrases used in this book. They are set off by italics in the text. Although not exhaustive, this glossary should come in handy for you and your shopping companions:

arrondissement. An administrative zone. Paris is divided into 20 arrondissements.

atelier. Workshop.

bar à vins. Wine bar.

batterie de cuisine. Kitchen equipment.

belle époque. Turn of the century.

bleus de travail. Blue cotton worker's uniform.

Bon Chic Bon Genre. Preppy younger generation.

bon ton. Good taste.

bonne affaire. Good deal.

boulettes grandmère. Chopped meatballs.

brocanteur. Secondhand dealer.

caleçons. Boxer shorts.

carnet. Small book of tickets or forms.

Carte Bleue. VISA card

chevrefeuille. Honeysuckle.

chez. At the house of.

chinoiserie. In the Chinese style.

choucroûte. Sauerkraut and sausage dish.

choux farcies. Stuffed cabbage rolls.

de rigueur. Required.

dégriffés. Labels taken out.

dégustation. Tasting.

dépôt vente. Resale establishment.

détaxe. Export discount.

doyenne. Eldest female of the group.

droite. Right.

duvet. Down comforter.

en vacances. On vacation.

Eurocarte. MasterCard.

faïence. Hand-painted earthenware.

fermé. Closed.

fermez. Please close.

fin de séries. End of the collection.

fin de siècle. End of the century.

flacon. Bottle, as for perfume.

flâner. Wander and browse.

foin coupé. Fresh cut hay.

folie. Something foolish.

fromage. Cheese.

galette. Pancake or flat cake.

gauche. Left.

givrette. Sugar-coated candy.

grand dame. Great lady.

grand magasin. Department store.

grandmère. Grandmother.

grêlon. Hailstone.

haricots fins. French green beans.

haute bourgeoisie. Upper middle class.

hôtel particulier. Private home.

joie de vivre. Love of life.

jardin. Garden.

jour de beauté. Day of beauty.

luxe. Luxury.

marché. Market.

marché aux puces. Flea markets.

métis. Fabric blend of linen and cotton.

mode feminine. Women's fashions.

mode moderne. Modern style.

montgolfiers. Hot air balloons.

ouvert. Open.

pain. Bread.

pain aux noix. Nut bread.

palais. Palace.

parfumerie. Perfume store.

petit rat. Young member of the ballet.

plat du jour. Plate of the day.

premier étage. First floor above the ground floor (2nd floor in U.S.)

prés. Fields.

quartier. Neighborhood.

Rallye. "Coming out" for young women.

rez-de-chausée. The ground floor (1st floor in U.S.)

Rive Droite. Right bank.

Rive Gauche. Left bank.

sachet. Packet.
santons. Traditional figurines representing the people of southern France.
savoir faire. Know-how.
soldes. Sale.
stock. Overstock.
tablier. Apron.
tapénade. Olive and anchovy spread.
tapisserie. Tapestry.
tarte tatin. Apple tart.
toque. Chef's hat.
tout. All.
trompe l'oeil. Deceptively real-looking.

Fashion Shop Talk

The following French words are all related to fashion:

à la mode. In style.
bas. Stockings.
bottine. Boot.
ceinture. Belt.
chaussures. Shoes.
couture. The clothing business.
cravate. Tie.
demi-couture. Made-to-measure clothing.
écharpe. Scarf.
fripes. Secondhand clothes.
gant. Glove.
haute couture. Custom sewn clothing from a fashion house which meets rigorous industry standards.
jupe. Skirt.
manteau. Coat.
pantalons. Pants.
peignoir. Nightgown.
prêt-à-porter. Ready-to-wear.
pullover. Sweater.
rétouchment. Alterations.
robe. Dress.
sac. Purse.
taille. Size.

Shop Talk Phrases

When you enter a small shop, engratiate yourself with a "Bonjour Madame." You will find the following phrases useful when you are shopping:

Do you accept credit cards or traveler's checks?
Acceptez-vous des cartes de crédit ou des chèques de voyages?

How much does this cost?
Ça coûte combien?

I would like the Export Sales Invoice for sales tax reimbursement.
Je voudrais l'imprimée pour la détaxe, s'il vous plaît.

Do you ship to the States?
Est-ce-que vous envoyez aux Etas-Unis?

I would like the package gift-wrapped.
Je voudrais un paquet cadeau, s'il vous plaît.

The Paris Shopping Companion will be updated for the next edition. If you find changes before I do or if you discover a shop you would like to see considered, please send me a note with your comments and any relevant information you may have. I welcome your feedback. Please send your comments to Susan Swire Winkler, c/o Cumberland House Publishing, 431 Harding Industrial Drive, Nashville, TN 37211.

Index

About the Author

Susan Swire Winkler was first fascinated by Paris as a young girl when she say the movie *Gigi*. Her experiences in Paris as a college student, graduate student, fashion journalist, and importer of French linens for her own shop allow her to view the city in a personal, authoritative way. A former writer for *Women's Wear Daily*, she lives in Portland, Oregon.